HELEN HUNT JACKSON

JACKSON

Selected Colorado Writings

D1599320

HELEN HUNT JACKSON

JACKSON

Selected Colorado Writings

Edited by

MARK I. WEST

FOR MY PARENTS, Carolyn and Walter West

MARK I. WEST was born in Colorado and grew up near Denver.
After receiving his Ph.D. in American Studies from Bowling Green State
University, he accepted a teaching position in the English Department
at the University of North Carolina at Charlotte. For ten years he served
as the Director of the American Studies Program. He currently holds
the position of Associate Dean for General Education. He has written
or edited twelve books, most of which deal with children's literature.

PHOTO CREDIT:
Cover photo: Helen Hunt Jackson, c. 1865
Courtesy: Colorado Springs Pioneers Museum.

LIBRARY OF CONGRESS CATALOGING-IN-PUBLICATION DATA
Jackson, Helen Hunt, 1830–1885.
  [Selections. 2002]
  Helen Hunt Jackson : selected Colorado writings /
edited by Mark West.
     p. cm.
  Includes bibliographical references.
  ISBN 0-86541-064-X
  1. Colorado—Literary collections. 2. Colorado—
Description and travel. I. West, Mark I. II. Title.
PS2106.W474 2002
818'.409—dc21

                                        2002151770

Printed in the United States
Copyright 2002 © Filter Press, LLC
DESIGN BY: F + P Graphic Design, Inc.

4

Contents

Portrait of Helen Hunt Jackson. From Poems by Helen Hunt Jackson *(Boston: Roberts Brothers, 1892).*

Acknowledgments

This book grew out of an extensive research project on Helen Hunt Jackson's Colorado writings, which was supported in part by funds provided by The University of North Carolina at Charlotte.

Throughout this project, I received valuable support and assistance from the staff of the Colorado Springs Pioneers Museum as well as the staff of the Special Collections Department of Colorado College's Tutt Library. My appreciation goes to all of these helpful people.

My thanks also go to my wife, Nancy Northcott, and our son, Gavin West. I could not ask for a more supportive family.

Helen Hunt Jackson's original gravesite on Cheyenne Mountain. Her body was moved to Evergreen Cemetery in Colorado Springs in 1891. From Poems by Helen Hunt Jackson *(Boston: Roberts Brothers, 1892).*

Introduction

Three years before Colorado's 1876 admission to the union, Helen Hunt Jackson (then known as Helen Hunt) moved from her native Massachusetts to Colorado Springs. Initially, she had no intention of becoming a permanent resident, but as it turned out, the town remained her primary residence until her death in 1885. Although she had achieved some success as a poet before moving west, her literary career blossomed during her Colorado years. Fifteen of the seventeen books that she published in her lifetime came out during this period, including two that deal directly with Colorado—*Bits of Travel at Home,* a collection of travel essays published in 1878, and *Nelly's Silver Mine: A Story of Colorado Life,* a novel for children also published in 1878.

Many of Jackson's books won acclaim from her contemporaries, but today she is primarily known for *Ramona,* her 1884 novel dealing with the plight of the California Mission Indians. Jackson's other book about Native Americans, *A Century of Dishonor: A Sketch of the United States Government's Dealings with Some of the Indian Tribes* (1881), is still read by historians, but the rest of her books have largely been forgotten.

Although Jackson has long ranked among Colorado's most famous authors, her writings about Colorado had been out of circulation for many years when I began my efforts to make these writings available to contemporay readers. In 1994, I edited a volume titled *Westward to a High Mountain: The Colorado Writings of Helen Hunt Jackson,* which was published by the Colorado Historical Society. This book brought back into print several of the essays from *Bits of Travel at Home* as well as an excerpt from *Nelly's Silver Mine.* I then edited *Bits of Colorado: Helen Hunt Jackson's Writings for Young Readers,* which Filter Press published in 2000. In this second volume I reprinted six pieces that Jackson intended for children.

Most of these pieces appeared first in children's periodicals and had never been published in a book. When W*estward to a High Mountain* went out of print, Doris Baker, publisher of Filter Press, suggested that I combine both collections into a single work, which is exactly what I have done in the present volume.

I believe that Jackson's Colorado writings are of historical and literary value and deserve attention from contemporary readers. The essays in *Bits of Travel at Home* provide first-hand accounts of the living conditions that faced the state's early settlers. These essays also contain some of the most vivid descriptions of the region's mountains, canyons, rock formations, and flora ever written. The Colorado pieces that she wrote for children help explain the appeal of early Colorado to ranchers, health-seekers, adventurers and naturalists. *Nelly's Silver Mine* should appeal to readers interested in the local color literary movement as well as those interested in the history of American children's literature. Although Jackson is not often classified as a local color writer, *Nelly's Silver Mine* provides amble evidence that she had a gift for capturing the nuances of life in a particular region. As a work of children's literature, *Nelly's Silver Mine* is worth reading for several reasons. Not only is it one of the first realistic children's books to be set in the West, but it also features a strong female protagonist, a fast-moving plot, and well-drawn secondary characters. For a nineteenth-century children's book, it is surprisingly free from didactic moralizing. Jackson also wrote poems about Colorado, two of which are included in this volume. These poems eloquently capture the spiritual side of Jackson's love of Colorado.

Jackson may never have fallen in love with Colorado or written much about the region if it were not for a suggestion made by her physician. In the fall of 1873, she was in poor health and sought her doctor's advice. He recommended that she spend the winter in Colorado Springs because he felt that the town's high altitude and low humidity would help her to regain her strength.[1]

The idea of uprooting herself and moving to a frontier town did not sound too appealing to her. At this point in her life, she was in her mid-forties and had already experienced much emotional upheaval. Her husband, Edward Bisell Hunt, had died in an accident in 1863. Her two sons had also died, one in infancy and the other at the age of nine. Given all the stress that she had been under, she was reluctant to take on the added stress of moving across the country. Furthermore, she felt quite at home in New England. She liked the historic quality of New England's towns, and she had many friends scattered around the region. If it were not for New England's damp winters, she would likely have ignored her doctor's advice. Ultimately, however, the attraction of escaping to a better climate convinced her to give Colorado Springs a try.

Traveling by train, she set out for Colorado in November 1873. When the train entered the Colorado Territory, she looked out her window and saw the vast flat land of the Great Plains. The sight left her cold. She described it as a "blank, bald, pitiless gray, under a gray November sky."[2] Her initial reactions to Colorado Springs were also negative. Because the town was only three years old, the buildings were so new that they looked raw to her. She wanted to turn around and go back to New England, but she had promised her doctor that she would stay for at least a month. She moved into the Colorado Springs Hotel, and before long her feelings toward Colorado started to change.

Just as her doctor had predicted, Colorado's climate agreed with her. Her health improved dramatically, and she soon felt well enough to take day trips around the area. She enjoyed exploring the cattle ranches and mining towns that surrounded Colorado Springs. What appealed to her the most, however, were the nearby mountains. She thrilled at the sight of Pikes Peak and Cheyenne Mountain, both of which practically shadow Colorado Springs. A canyon near Cheyenne Mountain became one of her favorite destinations. She described this canyon as a "great cathedral." On Sundays, she sometimes went to this canyon instead of going to church. As her affection for Colorado increased, she felt less and less homesick for New England.

Throughout her first year in Colorado, she used the Colorado Springs Hotel as her primary residence. Several other people also lived at the hotel, including a banker named William Sharpless Jackson. The two of them often saw each other, and before long they became friends. To some, their friendship seemed odd because they differed considerably in temperament. He was a practical-minded business-man who enjoyed large social gatherings while she was an intellectual who always avoided crowds. They shared, however, a love of the mountains and an interest in the lives of the pioneers who were settling in the area. As their friendship deepened, he began taking some of his afternoons off so that he could accompany her on her buggy rides through the countryside. One day he proposed to her. She was not sure she wanted to remarry, but she gradually warmed to the idea. On October 22, 1875, they were married, and from then on she was known as Helen Hunt Jackson.

Shortly before their marriage, William Jackson had purchased the most elegant house in Colorado Springs. Built in 1873, this Victorian house sat on the corner of Kiowa and Weber Streets. He had planned for the two of them to move into the house as soon as they were married, but his new wife insisted that they make major changes to the house first. She wanted the house reoriented so that it would face the mountains rather than the prairie. To achieve this goal, the Jacksons arranged to have the house rebuilt. It took many months of work, but when the renovations were complete, Helen Hunt Jackson could look out the front windows and see her beloved Cheyenne Mountain.

She took great pleasure in decorating their new home. She had shelves and cupboards installed in practically every corner of every room, and she filled them all with books, vases, sculptures, Indian baskets, and various other objects that she had collected during her travels. She decorated the numerous mantelpieces with wild flowers and kinnikinnick that she regularly gathered when she took her afternoon excursions into the mountains. She covered the walls with paintings and the floors with Oriental rugs. Visitors often thought that the house looked too cluttered, but she liked its appearance. For the first time in years, she felt as if she truly had a home of her own.[3]

Jackson generally wrote in one of the front rooms, where she could enjoy the view. Given her love of the mountains, it is not surprising that many of the first pieces she wrote in her new home were descriptive essays about the Colorado mountains. She focused some essays, however, on particular towns, such as Colorado Springs or the mining town of Rosita. In other essays, she chronicled the experiences she had during her excursions through the Rockies. These sketches ran in several prominent eastern magazines, including *Atlantic Monthly, New York Independent,* and *Scribner's Monthly.*

In 1878, Jackson pulled together her Colorado travel sketches along with some essays about her travels in New England and California and sent them off to Roberts Brothers, the Boston publishing firm that brought out most of her books. Later that year, Roberts Brothers published these essays in a volume entitled *Bits of Travel at Home.* The book received many positive reviews, including a rave review in the *Hartford Courant.*[4] Like many other reviewers of the book, the author of this review was especially impressed with the Colorado essays:

> Nearly half of the volume is given to Colorado, and the frontispiece is a view of Colorado Springs, with its background of snow mountains, where the author lives. She is a fervent apostle of her new home, and if any body can convince the east that it is a Paradise to live in, and cause a rush of settlers to it, it is the persuasive author of this volume. Next to the loadstone of its mineral wealth, we verily believe that Colorado owes a chief debt for its good reputation to its best known and most distinguished citizen.[5]

In most of her travel sketches, Jackson focused on the state's natural features rather than on its residents. As she came to know the people of Colorado better, she decided to write a children's book in which the emphasis would be on the pioneers who settled the area. This decision led her to write *Nelly's Silver Mine: A Story of Colorado Life*, her first and only novel for children. She began writing the novel, according to a note she made in her diary, on July 9, 1877.[6] Roberts Brothers offered her a contract for the book in March 1878 and published it later that year.

The central characters in *Nelly's Silver Mine* are Mr. and Mrs. March and their twelve-year-old twins, Nelly and Rob. The March family, like Jackson, is from Massachusetts. The family decides to move to Colorado at the recommendation of their doctor, who feels that Colorado's low humidity will help cure Mr. March's asthma. At first, the children do not want to leave their home, but their reservations evaporate as soon as Mr. March shows them stereoscopic pictures of Pikes Peak and other scenes from Colorado.

Just as Jackson had done, the March family travels to Denver by train and then boards another train for Colorado Springs. The train scenes perfectly capture the realities of traveling by rail during the 1870s. The passanger cars are filled with immigrants from several European countries, health seekers from New England, and a scattering of adventurers who want to see the Wild West. As the train makes its ways across the Great Plains, the tension among this disparate collection of people continually escalates. Jackson's depiction of the conflicts among the passengers goes a long way toward dispelling the romanticism often associated with train travel.

Once the March family arrives in Colorado Springs, they go by wagon to a mountain ranch near the small town of Manitou Springs. The children take an instant liking to their new environment, and Mr. March's asthma completely disappears. Not everything, however, goes well for the March family. As was often the case with novice ranchers, they lose more money than they make. They finally give up and move to another ranch that is located south of Colorado Springs in a sheltered valley. During their first year on the new ranch, they prosper, but the next year their crops are destroyed by grasshoppers. The children worry about the family's finances and try to help out by selling butter and eggs to the residents of a nearby town.

Although the March family sticks to ranching, many of their neighbors try to make a living by mining silver. Nelly and Rob become obsessed with the idea of finding their own silver mine. They learn everything they can about mining, including how to determine which areas are worth investigating. In one of the most exciting scenes in the story, Nelly locates a spot that looks like it's going to be rich in silver ore.

Nelly's Silver Mine includes lots of factual information about ranching and silver mining, but this material is carefully woven into the plot. In writing the book, Jackson drew heavily on her many discussions with the ranchers and miners who lived in and around Colorado Springs. Thus, even though she never pursued either of these occupations herself, she was able to provide a balanced and accurate portrayal of these settlers' experiences.

The book's realism won praise from many reviewers. Several pointed out that Jackson's description of frontier life was much more convincing than the depiction found in the popular dime-novel westerns. These reviewers were pleased that Jackson portrayed the settlers as hard workers rather than as a bunch of wild desperadoes. As the reviewer for *Atlantic Monthly* put it, "The story of *Nelly's Silver Mine* comes as a grateful relief from the literature for the young which deals with the more barbaric side of Western frontier life."[7]

Shortly after the publication of *Nelly's Silver Mine*, Jackson began challenging another dime-novel stereotype—the savage Indian. Jackson's experiences in Colorado led her to become concerned about the misconceptions surrounding Native Americans. During the late 1860s and 1870s, Colorado was the site of a major conflict between the settlers and the Utes. Jackson had hardly been aware of this conflict when she first moved to Colorado Springs, but her research into the history of the region brought this matter to her attention. She learned that government officials often used racist stereotypes in order to justify the killing and relocation of the Utes.[8] This injustice troubled her, but it was not until 1879 that she decided to take a public stand on the "Indian question." She made this decision after listening to a Ponca chief named Standing Bear give a speech about the suffering of the Plains Indians.[9]

Jackson's growing concern about the mistreatment of Native Americans resulted in a shift in her writing career. From 1879 until her death in 1885, she devoted most of her publications to the cause of winning public support and sympathy for Native Americans. This new commitment, however, did not mean that she stopped writing about Colorado altogether. During this period, she wrote several more Colorado travel sketches, a number of articles about Colorado history and life for the children's magazine *Youth's Companion.*

While Jackson was conducting the research for *Ramona,* she spent much of her time in southern California, which is where the book is set. She still, though, thought of Colorado as her home. Soon after the 1884 publication of *Ramona,* she rejoined her husband in Colorado Springs and set about redecorating their house. On June 28, 1884, she was climbing the stairs in the house when she fell and broke her hip. Her doctors ordered her to rest until her hip healed and her strength returned. As the months passed, however, it became clear that she was suffering from more than a broken hip. Hoping that a change in climate might help, she went to San Francisco. While there, she learned that she had cancer. Her husband joined her on August 2, 1885, and she died ten days later.

Before her death, she had requested that her body be buried on Cheyenne Mountain. Mr. Jackson honored her request, but six years later he reluctantly agreed to have her body moved to a cemetery in Colorado Springs because the first gravesite was too out-of-the-way to tend properly. Although her body no longer rests in the mountains, surely her spirit always will.

Notes

1. For more information about Jackson's move west and her life in Colorado see Ruth Odell, *Helen Hunt Jackson* (New York: D. Appleton-Century Co., 1939), 130-50. See also Evelyn I. Banning, *Helen Hunt Jackson* (New York: Vanguard Press, 1973), 98-134.

2. Qtd. in Odell, 130.

3. For more information about Jackson's home in Colorado Springs see Mark I. West, *Wellsprings of Imagination: The Homes of Children's Authors* (New York: Neal-Schuman, 1992), 46-54.

4. Odell implies that *Bits of Travel at Home* received mostly negative reviews (134–35). My research does not support this conclusion. The book received a few negative reviews, one of which Odell cites, but the great majority of them were very favorable.

5. This review is included in the Helen Hunt Jackson Collection at Colorado College's Tutt Library in Colorado Springs. The exact date of the review is not provided.

6. Jackson's diary is included in the Helen Hunt Jackson Collection at Colorado College's Tutt Library.

7. "Recent Literature," *Atlantic Monthly,* December 1878, 779.

8. Virginia McConnell, "H.H., Colorado, and the Indian Problem," *Journal of the West,* 7, No. 2 (1973), 272-280.

9. For more information about Jackson's writings about Native Americans see Valerie Sherer Mathes, *Helen Hunt Jackson and Her Indian Reform Legacy* (Austin: University of Texas Press, 1990). For examples of the letters she wrote on this topic, see Valerie Sherer Mathes, *The Indian Reform Letters of Helen Hunt Jackson, 1879-1885* (Norman: University of Oklahoma Press, 1998).

Colorado Springs

Jackson wrote this essay a little over seven months after moving to Colorado Springs. In addition to extolling the virtues of her new home town, she devoted part of this essay to describing the beauty of the surrounding countryside. "Colorado Springs" first appeared in the August 13, 1874, issue of the NEW YORK INDEPENDENT.

I once said of a face, at hasty first sight, "What a plain face! How is it that people have called it handsome? I see no single point of beauty in it."

That face afterward became in my eyes not only noble, fine, strong, sweet, but beautiful, apart from its beauty as an index and record of the loveliest nature and life I have ever known. Again and again I try to recall the face as I first saw it. I cannot. The very lineaments seem totally changed.

It is much the same with my first impression of the Colorado Springs. I shall never forget my sudden sense of hopeless disappointment at the moment when I first looked on the town. It was a gray day in November. I had crossed the continent, ill, disheartened, to find a climate which would not kill. There stretched before me, to the east, a bleak, bare, unrelieved, desolate plain. There rose behind me, to the west, a dark range of mountains, snow-topped, rocky-walled, stern, cruel, relentless. Between lay the town—small, straight, new, treeless.

"One might die of such a place alone," I said bitterly. "Death by disease would be more natural."

To-day that plain and those mountains are to me well nigh the fairest spot on earth. To-day I say, "One might almost live on such a place alone." I have learned it, as I learned that human face, by heart; and there can be a heart and a significant record in the face of a plain and a mountain, as much as in the face of a man.

To those who care to know the position of Colorado Springs geographically, it can be said that its latitude is about the same as that of Washington City; that it lies in El Paso County, seventy miles to the south of Denver and five miles from the foot of Pike's Peak. For myself and for those whom I might possibly win to love Colorado Springs as I love it, I would say simply that it is a town lying due east of the Great Mountains and west of the sun.

Again, to those who are curious as to statistics and dates and histories of affairs, it might be said that three years ago the town of Colorado Springs did not exist, and that to-day it numbers three thousand inhabitants; that it is also known as the "Fountain Colony,"—a name much more attractive than Colorado Springs, and also more fitting for the place, since there is not a spring of any sort whatever in the town, and the soda and chalybeate springs, which have done so much to make the region famous, are five miles away, in the town of Manitou.

The trustees of the Fountain Colony are men of means, position, and great executive ability. What is more, they are enthusiasts,—enthusiasts in their faith in the future of this region, and enthusiasts in their determination to exert their controlling power in the right direction. They hold in their jurisdiction a tract of about ten thousand acres of land; and the money derived from the sales of two-thirds of this property is to be and is being expended in the construction of irrigating canals, roads, parks, schools, the planting of trees, and other improvements. All deeds contain an improvement clause, and a clause prohibiting the manufacture or sale of intoxicating liquors on the property. Already the liquor-dealers and the company have come into collision, and the contest will wax hotter, no doubt; but the company is resolved that the town shall continue to be, as it began, a temperance town, and it will be an evil day for the little village if ever the whiskey dealers and drinkers win the fight.

The streets of the town are laid out at right angles and are alternately one hundred and one hundred and forty feet wide.

Narrow streams of running water are carried through all the streets, as in Salt Lake City. Cottonwood trees have been planted regularly along these little streams. Already these trees are large enough to give some shade. Already there are in the town, bakeries, laundries, livery stables, billiard halls, restaurants, mills, shops, hotels, and churches. In all these respects, the town is far better provided than the average New England town of the same population. Remoteness from centres of supplies compels towns, as it compels individuals, to take care of themselves.

These things I mention for the sake of those who are anxious as to statistics, and dates, and the history of affairs. There is much more of the same sort that might be told; of the great increase in the value of property, for instance, lots having trebled in value within six months; of the great success in stock-raising in this region, the herds running free on the plains all winter long, requiring no shelter, and feeding well on the dry sweet grasses; of the marvellous curative qualities of the climate,—asthma, throat diseases, and earlier stages of consumption being, almost without exception, cured by this dry and rarefied air. But all these things are set forth in the circulars of the Fountain Colony, in the reports of medical associations, and in pamphlets and treatises on Western immigration and the future of Colorado,—set forth accurately, even eloquently. The statistician, the pioneer, the builder of railroads, has his own language, his own sphere; and to him one must go for the facts of a country, for the catalogue of its resources, the forecasting of its destiny. But it is perhaps also worth while to look at a lover's portrait of it. A picture has uses, as well as a gazetteer. There is more stimulus sometimes in suggestion than in information; more delight in the afterglow of reminiscence than in the clear detail of observation. For myself, therefore, and for those along whom I might possibly win to love Colorado Springs as I love it, I repeat that it is a town lying east of the Great Mountains and west of the sun. Between it and the morning sun and between it and the far southern horizon stretch plains which have all the beauty of the sea added to the beauty of

plains. Like the sea they are ever changing in color, and seem illimitable in distance. But they are full of tender undulations and curves,
which never vary except by light and shade. They are threaded here
and there by narrow creeks, whose course is revealed by slender,
winding lines of cottonwood trees, dark green in summer, and in
winter of a soft, clear gray, more beautiful still. They are broken
here and there by sudden rises of table-lands, sometimes abrupt,
sharpsided, and rocky, looking like huge castles or lines of fortifica-
tions; sometimes soft, mound-like, and imperceptibly widening,
like a second narrow tier of plain overlying the first.

The sloping side of these belts of table-land are rifted and
hollowed and fluted endlessly. Miniature canyons, filled with green
growths, nooks and dells, and overlapping mounds, make up the
mystery of their beauty. Water-washed stones and honeycombed
rocks are strewed on many of them, showing that their shapes were
founded ages ago by mighty waves. No wonder, then, that these
plains add, as I said, to the beauty of plains all the beauty of the sea.
Their surface is covered with close, low grasses,—amber brown,
golden yellow, and claret red in winter; in summer of a pale olive
green, far less beautiful, vivid, and vitalized than the browns and
yellows and reds of the winter. But in the summer come myriads of
flowers, lighting up the olive green background, making it into a
mosaic of white and purple and pink and scarlet and yellow.
Smooth, hard roads cross these plains, north, south, east, west, without turning, without guide-post, without landmark; many of them
seeming so aimless, endless, that one wonders why they are there at
all. It takes but a few times driving anywhere to mark out a road. If
a ditch overflows and a gully is made, the next half dozen passers-by
drive a little to the right or left; the new road is begun and practically made, and after a few mornings purple vetches and daisies will
be blossoming in the old one. Looking northward over this sea-plain,
one sees at the horizon a dark blue line, like a wall, straight, even-
topped, unbroken. This is the "Divide,"—another broad-spreading
belt of table-land, lifting suddenly from the plains, running from

east to west, and separating them. Its highest point is eight thousand feet above the sea, and is crossed by the Denver and Rio Grande Railroad. On its very summit lies a lake, whose shores in June are like garden-beds of flowers, and in October are blazing with the colors of rubies and carnelians.

It is a gracious and beautiful country the Divide, eight or ten miles in width and seventy long, well wooded and watered, and with countless glens and valleys full of castellated rocks and pine groves. All this one learns journeying across it; but, looking up at it from Colorado Springs, it is simply a majestic wall against the northern sky,—blue, deep, dark, unfathomable blue, as an ocean wave might be if suddenly arrested at its highest and crystallized into a changeless and eternal boundary. It is thirty or forty miles away from us; but in every view we find our eyes fastening upon it, tracing it, wondering how, not being built of *lapis lazuli* or clouded sapphire, it can be so blue. It is the only spot in our glorious outlook which is uniform of color. Sunsets may turn the whole north sky golden yellow, and the afterglow may stretch rosy red the entire circle round, while the plains below fade from brilliant sunlight to soft, undistinguishable gray; but the wall of the Divide remains always of its own unchanging blue. Storms sweep over it, black and fierce, but the blue shows through. Snow covers it and the winter sky arches white above it, but still its forest ranks of pines and firs stand solid, constant blue in the horizon. This is a dim picture of what we who dwell in this town east of the mountains and west of the sun see when we look south and east or north,— a very dim picture, since it set forth only the shapes and proportions, and can in no wise suggest the colors. If I say that even on this day (the two hundred and eleventh day that I have looked on these plains) I see colors and combinations of colors I never saw before, and that out of the two hundred and eleven days there have been no two days alike, who will believe me? No one,—perhaps not even they who have dwelt by my side; yet it is true, and a calendar there would be records of days when the whole plain looked like a soft floor of gray mist, its mounds and hills of vapor, slow curling and rounding; when it looked like a floor of beaten gold, even, solid, shining; or like a tapestry, too, for the bands are ever shifting, deepening, paling, advancing, receding, vanishing and coming again, as the clouds come or go, deepen or pale, in the skies above; or, if it be winter, like a trackless, illimitable, frozen ocean, with here and there dark icebergs looming up. Not the furthest Polar Sea can look like wider, icier Arctic space than does this sunny plain when it is white with snow.

In such calendar there would be records of hours when, in spite of the whole sunset plains being darkened by overhanging clouds, the sunlight floods every bluff and castellated mound in the east, lifting them and making them look like fairy realms, with spires and slopes and turreted walls of gold; of hours again when the plains, being in strong, full light, clouds chance to rest above the same bluffs, transforming them into grim and dark and terrible fortresses, bearing no semblance to the smiling fairy castles of gold they were the day before; of hours on some winter morning, when every tiny grass-blade, flower-stalk, and shrub on the whole plain has been covered with snow crystals in the night,—not with the common round feathery crystals, but with acicular crystals fine as a cobweb thread, an inch or an inch and a half long, and so close set that even stout weed-stalks curve and bend under the weight of their snowy fringe. Upon these myriads, acres, miles of crystals flashes the hot sun, and almost in the twinkling of an eye the plain changes from soft and solid white to a field of glistening sparkles, and from the glistening sparkles back to its pale yellows and browns. Even in the few seconds while I have been walking past an oak shrub I have seen every dried leaf on it change from white to brown, so marvellous is this Colorado sun,—its direct rays burning as through a burning-glass. There would be records of hours when having gone a few hundred feet up on the eastward slope of Cheyenne Mountain, we sat down in a fragrant garden of gillias, scarlet penstemons, spiraeas, wild roses, columbines, red lilies, lupines, harebells, and myriads more which we knew not, and looked off over the plains. Though they were only three or four miles away, they looked as if we might journey for days and not reach them,—so wide, so remote, so deep down, so ineffably soft and misty. We sat, as I say, in a garden; but there was in the garden, besides the flowers, a confusion of great rocks and oak bushes and tall pines and firs. There were no level spaces, only nooks between rocks and here and there zigzag intervals: but on every inch of ground some green or flowering thing grew; ravines, with unsuspected brooks in them, were on each hand. Parting the tangles of bushes and creeping or springing down their sides, we found great clumps of golden and white columbines and green ferns.

Between the pines and firs were wonderful vistas of the radiant plain. Each glimpse was a picture in itself,—now an open space of clear, sunny distance; now a belt of cottonwood trees, making a dark green oasis in the yellow; now the majestic bluffs, looking still more castlelike, framed in the dark foreground lines of pine boughs. We were in shadow. The sun had set for us; but it was yet early afternoon on the plain and it was brilliant with sun. As we went slowly down, bearing our sheaves of flowers, the brilliance slowly faded, and the lower sunset light cast soft shadow on every mound and hill and hollow. The whole plain seemed dimpling with shadows; each instant they deepened and moved eastward; first revealing and then slowly hiding each rise and fall in the vast surface. Away in the east, sharply against the sky, lines of rocky bluffs gleamed white as city walls; close at the base of the mountain the foot-hills seemed multiplied and transfigured into countless velvet mounds. The horizon line seemed to curve more and more, as if somehow the twilight were folding the world up for night, and we were on some outside shore watching it. One long, low cloud lay in amber and pink bars above the blue wall of the Divide, a vivid rosy band of afterglow spread slowly in the east and south; and the town below us looked strangely like an army, with its wide avenues and battalion-like parallelograms of houses.

If I have dwelt long on what one sees looking north, east, south from Colorado Springs, it is not because the westward outlook

—I had almost said uplook—is less grand, less satisfying; rather because the reverent love for mountains is like a reverent love for a human being,—reticent, afraid of the presumptuousness of speech.

Looking westward, we see only mountains. Their summits are in the skies, ten, twelve, fourteen thousand feet high. Their foot-hills and foot-hill slopes reach almost to the base of the plateau on which the town stands. Whether the summits or the foot-hills are more beautiful one forever wonders and is never sure. The summits are sharp, some of them of bare red rock, gleaming under the summer sunrise like pyramids of solid garnet, yet blue again at sunset,—of a purple blue, as soft as the purple blue of grapes at their ripest. Sometimes in winter, they are more beautiful still,—so spotless white, stately, and solemn that if one believes there is a city of angels he must believe that these are the towers and gates thereof.

The foot-hills are closely grown with grass. In winter they are, like the prairies, brown and yellow and claret, varying in tint and shade, according to the different growths and in every shifting light from sunrise to sunset. No one who has not seen can fancy the beauty of a belt of such colors as these at base of mountains of red and yellow sandstone. The foothills lap and overlap and interrupt each other, sometimes repeating in softened miniature the outline of the crowding and overlapping peaks above. Here and there sharp ridges of sandstone rock have been thrown up among them. The spaces between these are so hollowed and smooth-moulded that they look like beautiful terraced valleys, with jagged red walls on either hand. When sunset casts alternate beams of light and shade across these valleys, and the red walls glow redder and redder, they look like veritable enchanted lands; and if one looks up to the snow-topped mountains above the sense of enchantment is only heightened. And this is what Colorado Springs sees, looking west. Are there many spots on earth where the whole rounded horizon is thus full of beauty and grandeur, and where to all the grandeur of outline and beauty of color is added the subtle and indescribable spell of the rarefied air and light of six thousand feet above the sea?

One day last winter we saw a prismatic cloud in the sky. It was high noon. The cloud lay close to the sun: it was fleecy, yet solid; white, yet brilliant with all the rainbow tints of mother-of-pearl. All who saw it held their breaths with a sense of something preternatural in its beauty. Every instant the tints changed. They paled, they deepened, they shifted place,—pink, yellow, green, separate, blended, iridescent. As one holds up a mother-of-pearl shell to the light, turning it slowly back and forth to catch the rays, it seemed as if some invisible hand must be holding up this shining cloud and moving it slowly back and forth in the sun. The wonderful spectacle lasted some ten minutes; then slowly the iridescence disappeared, leaving the cloud simply a white and fleecy cloud, like myriads of others in the sky. It seemed to me emblematic of the beauty of this whole panorama, which has as mystical a quality of endless change as the iridescent tints of mother-of-pearl. While light lasts never shall mother-of-pearl show twice exactly the same harmony, exactly the same succession of tints. And I believe that hour after hour, day after day, and year after year, these plains and mountains will never show twice the same harmony, the same succession. Most earnestly I believe, also, that there is to be born of these plains and mountains, all along the great central plateaus of continent, the very best life, physical and mental, of the coming centuries. There are to be patriarchal families living with their herds, as patriarchs lived of old on the eastern plains. Of such life, such blood, comes culture a few generations later,—a culture all the better because it comes spontaneously and not of effort, is a growth and not a graft. It was in the east that the wise men saw the star; but it was westward to a high mountain, in a lonely place, that the disciples were led for the transfiguration!

North Cheyenne Cañon. From The Crest of the Continent
(Chicago: R.R. Donnelly and Sons, 1885).

A Colorado Week

In this essay, Jackson chronicled a week-long excursion that she and three friends took through the mountains in July 1874. They traveled from Colorado Springs to South Park and back again. Along the way they went through Ute Pass, visited the mining town of Fairplay, and climbed to the summit of Mount Lincoln. This essay originally ran as a four-part series in the NEW YORK INDEPENDENT *in October 1874.*

Only from Saturday to Saturday, and I suppose the days could not have been more than twenty-four hours long; but what a week it was! Ten hours a day out under a Colorado sky; ten hours a day of Colorado mountain air; ten hours a day of ever-changing delight; beauty deepening to grandeur, grandeur softening to beauty, and beauty and grandeur together blending in pictures which no pencil, no pen can render,—pictures born only to be stamped upon hearts, never to be transferred to canvas or to page. I said that the days could not have been more than twenty-four hours long. I spoke hastily, and am not at all sure of any thing of the kind. There is a comic story of a traveller in Colorado who, having been repeatedly misled and mystified by the marvellous discrepancies between real and apparent distances in the rarefied air, was found one day taking off his shoes and stockings to wade through a little brook, not a foot wide.

"Why, man, what are you about? Why don't you step over?" exclaimed everybody.

He shook his head and continued his preparations for wading.

"No! no! you can't fool me," he exclaimed. "I shan't be surprised if it turns out to be a quarter of a mile across this brook."

One comes to have much the same feeling about outdoor days in Colorado. Enjoyment can be rarefied, like air, so that its measures of time grow meaningless and seem false, as do the measures of distance in the upper air. I am not in the least sure, therefore, that these days of which I write were only twenty-four hours long. I do know, however, that it was on a Saturday we set out, and on the next Saturday we came home, and that the week might be called the Holy Week of our summer.

We set out at noon from Colorado Springs. Thirty-five miles, chiefly up-hill miles, were to be driven before night. The seven hours would be none too long. As we drove through the busy streets of the little town, hearty "good-byes" and "good-times to you" came from friend after friend, on the sidewalk or in the doorways. Not the least among the charms of the simple life in this far new West is the out-spoken interest and sympathy between neighbors. That each man knows what each other man does or is going to do becomes an offence or a pleasure according to the measures of good will involved in the curiosity and familiarity. In older communities people have crystallized into a strong indifference to each other's affairs, which, if it were analyzed, would be found to be nine parts selfishness. In the primitive conditions of young colonies this is impossible. Helpfulness and sympathy are born of the hard-pressing common needs and the closely-linked common life. The hearty, confiding, questioning, garrulous speech of the Western American really has its source in a deep substratum of this kindly sympathy. It sounds odd and unpleasant enough, no doubt, to Eastern ears and tried by the Eastern standards of good manners; but, reflecting on it, one comes to do it a tardy justice and meet it on its own ground fairly and with honest liking. All this I thought as, driving out of Colorado Springs that Saturday noon, we passed many persons who, although they knew only one of our party, were evidently well aware that we were setting out for the mountains, waved their hands and smiled and called out: "Good-bye, good-bye. A good trip to you." Who shall say that the influence of such cheery benedictions from friendly hearts does not last far beyond the moment in which they are spoken; does not enter into one's good luck, by some moral chemistry subtler than any for which the material science can find analysis or formula? The world would be none the worse for believing this, at any rate, and we should all be friendlier and readier and freer in greetings.

Thirty-five miles westward and up-hill we drove that afternoon, through the lovely nestled nook of Manitou and up the grand Ute Pass. The oftener one goes through this pass, the grander it seems. There are in it no mere semblances, no delusions of atmospheric effect. It is as severely, sternly real as Gibraltar. Sunlight cannot soften it nor storms make it more frowning. High, rocky, inaccessible, its walls tower and wind and seem at every turn to close rather than to open the path through which the merry little stream comes leaping, foaming down. The rocks on either side are scarred and grooved and seamed and wrought, as if the centuries had rent asunder some giant fortress, but found slender triumph in its fall,—two fortresses being set now to guard the spot where before there had been but one. The contrast is sharp and weird between the sparkling amber and white brook, paved with shining pebbles and shaded by tangled growths of willows and clematis and tasselled festoons of wild hops, and the bare red and gray rock walls, rising hundreds and hundreds of feet, unrelieved except by straight, stern, dark, unyielding firs,— so sharp, so weird a contrast that one unconsciously invests both the brook and the rock walls above with a living personality and antagonism, and longs that the brook should escape. For a short distance the road is narrow and perilous—on strips of ledges between two precipices, or on stony rims of the crowded brook, which it crosses and recrosses twenty-four times in less than three miles. Then the Pass widens, the rocky walls sink gradually, round and expand into lovely hills—hill after hill, bearing more and more off to the right and more and more off to the left—until there is room for bits of meadow along the brook and for groves and grassy intervals where the hills join; room and at the same time shelter, for the hills are still high. And that their slopes are sunny and warm in the early spring we find record written in clumps of the waving seed-vessels of the beautiful blue wind-flower of Colorado, the *Anemone patens.* In April, if we had been here, we should have seen these slopes blue with the lovely cup-blossoms. Except in color, the seed-vessels are no less beautiful. Fancy a dandelion seedglobe with each one of its downy spokes expanded into a hairy plume two inches or two and a half in length, the soft gray hairs set thick on both sides the tiny centre thread, regular as on an ostrich feather and fine as the down on a butterfly's wing. I have one before me as I write. It was overripe when I gathered it. The plumes had been blown and twisted by the wind, till no two are alike in their curve or direction. Yet it is still a globe; a dainty dishevelled little curly-head of a thing, by whose side the finest dandelion "blow" would look stupid and set and priggish. Out of curiosity—not idle, but reverent—I set myself to counting the plumes. They were tangled, so that it was not easy. I counted twelve springing from a pin's-point centre. There must be a hundred or more in all. But I left off counting, for it seemed like a cruel pulling of a baby's hair.

It was nightfall when we reached the ranch at which we were to sleep. We had climbed several divides, rising, falling, rising, falling, all in the depths of pine forests, all steadily mounting westward, toward the great central range; and we came out at sunset on a ridge from which we could look down into a meadow. The ridge sloped down to the meadow through a gateway made by two huge masses of rocks. All alone in the smooth grassy forest, they loomed up in the dim light, stately and straight as colossal monoliths, though they were in reality composed of rounded bowlders piled one above another. Because they are two and alone and set over against each other, men have called them The Twins. All over the world, even among the most uncultured people, we find this unconscious investiture of Nature with personality, so instinctive a tendency have sensitive hearts toward a noble and tender pantheism.

As we paused on this ridge, the western sky was filled with red sunset clouds; the western horizon was one long line of dark blue mountain peaks, seeming to uphold the red canopy of clouds. Only at the point of the sun's sinking was there a golden tint. There two blue peaks stood sharply outlined against a vivid yellow sky;

one fine line of gold, like an arch, spanned the interval and linked the peaks together. The magic bridge lasted but a second; before we had fully caught the beautiful sight, arch and yellow sea and blue peaks together were all swimming in rosy clouds.

The ranch was a cluster of log cabins. When the Colorado ranchman prospers, his log cabins multiply and grow out from and on to one another, very much as barnacles spread and congregate on a rock. At foot of a hill and spreading up on its side, such a log-cabin clump is a wonderfully picturesque sight. The irregular white plaster lines in all the crevices between the brown logs; the yellow hewn ends interlocked at the corners; the low doors, square windows, and perhaps flat roof, with grass waving on it,—altogether the picture is not unpleasing, and is beautiful compared with that of the average small frame house,—high, straight, sharpangled, narrow-roofed, abominable. On entering, you will probably find the walls and ceiling papered with old newspapers. The ultimate intent of illustrated weeklies flashes instantly clear on one's comprehension. They may be forgiven for existing. To the dwellers in log cabins they are priceless. I have seen in rich men's houses far uglier wall-papers than they make, and there is endless entertainment in lying in bed of a morning and reading up and down and across your bed-room walls that sort of verse which is printed in the "Blades" and "Flags" and "Spirits" and "Times" of our Union.

When we first looked to the west the next morning the two peaks which had been blue the night before and circled by the fine line of gold were deep gray on a faint pink sky. Our road lay directly toward them. "All day we shall see," we said, "the mystic gold arch spanning the space between them, as we saw it in yesterday's sunset." But we did not. Sufficient unto the day is the beauty thereof in Colorado. One does not remember nor anticipate the beauties of yesterday or tomorrow. The gold arch was forgotten before we had driven half an hour through the meadows of flowers. Great patches of brilliant fire-weed on all sides. On the road edges, rims of a fine feathery white flower, new to us all; dainty wild flax, its blue disks waving and nodding; clumps of scarlet "painter's-brush" gleaming out like red torches in the grass; tall spikes of white and pink and scarlet gilia; and everywhere, making almost a latticed setting for the rest, mats and spikes and bushes of yellow blossoms. Six different kinds of yellow flowers we counted; but, shame to us, we knew the names of no one of them.

On a knoll in the meadows, within stone's throw of the sluggish Platte River, yet well sheltered by wooded hills on two sides, stood a small frame house,—the house of a famous old hunter. Deer-skins and fox-skins were drying on the fences; huge elk-horns leaned against the sides of the house. As we drove slowly by, the old man came out. His hair was white and his face thickly wrinkled; but his eye was bright, clear, and twinkling with gladness and energy, like the gladness and energy of youth.

"Never go out but what I bring home something, sir,—an antelope, if nothing more," he said, in reply to a question as to the hunting in the neighborhood. Summer and winter the old man ranges the hills and his name is well known in the markets of Denver and Colorado Springs.

Leaving the Platte meadows, we began to climb hills to the west. Divide after divide, like those we climbed and crossed the day before, we climbed now. Still the Great Range stood apparently as far off as ever. From the tops of all the ridges we looked off to it, and looking backward, saw Pike's Peak making as high and majestic a wall in the east. The hills were so alike, the distance so apparently undiminished that we began to feel as if we were in an enchantment,—living over a "Story without an End," in which we should wander for ever in a succession of pine-covered ridges and valleys, lured on by an endlessly retreating wall of snow-topped mountains before us. But an end came; that is, an end to the pinecovered ridges. It was an end which was a beginning, however. Shall we ever forget the moment when, having climbed the highest of the pine-covered ridges, we found ourselves on a true summit at last, on the summit of the eastern wall of the great South Park.

The South Park is sixty miles long and forty wide, a majestic, mountain-walled valley; a valley eight or nine thousand feet high. Its extreme western wall is the great central range of the Rocky Mountains, but so many lesser ranges are massed and built up against this that the effect to the eye is as if there lay only mountains to the very outermost edge of the world. To the north and to the south it is the same. We looked down on this valley from near the centre of the eastern ridges. The view had the vastness of a view from a high mountain peak, mingled with the beauty of one from near hills. A great silence, like the great silence of the place, fell upon us. The scene seemed almost unreal. From our very feet to the distant western wall, forty miles away, stretched the soft, smooth, olive-gray surface of the valley, with belts and bars and flickering spaces of dark shadows of yellow sunlight playing over it.

Here and there rose hills,—some wooded, some bare and of the same soft olive-gray of the valley. Some were almost high enough to be called mountains; some were low and fluted in smooth water-worn grooves. These were islands when South Park was a lake. They looked hardly less like islands now, and the olive-gray plain when it was a placid sea could not have had a smoother tint or a tenderer light on its shimmering surface. The dome of the sky looked strangely vast and high. It was filled with fleecy, shifting clouds and its blue was unfathomably deep. There seemed no defined horizon to west or south or north; only a great outlying continent of mountain peaks, bounding, upholding, and piercing the dome above it. There was no sound, no sight, no trace of human life. The silence, the sense of space in these Rocky Mountains solitudes cannot be expressed; neither can the peculiar atmospheric beauty be described. It is the result partly of the grand distances, partly of the rarefied air. The shapes are the shapes of the north, but the air is like the air of the tropics,—shimmering, kindling. No pictures of the Rocky Mountains which I have seen have caught it in the least. There is not a cold tint here. No dome of Constantinople or Venice, no pyramid of Egypt, ever glowed and swam in warmer light and of warmer hue than do these colossal mountains. Some mysterious secret of summer underlies and outshines their perpetual snows. Perhaps it is only the ineffable secret of distance. Nowhere else in the world are there mountains fourteen and fifteen thousand feet high which have all the room they need,—great circles and semicircles of plains at their feet and slopes a half continent long!

As we drove down into the valley, the horizon peaks slowly sank; with each mile they changed place, lessened, disappeared, until only the loftiest ones remained in sight. Winding among the hills, which had looked from the summit of the valley like isolated islands, we found them sometimes linked together by long divides, which we climbed and crossed, as we had those of the valley walls. With each of these lifts came a fresh view of the myriad mountains around us. Then we sank again to the lower level, and the plain seemed again to stretch endlessly before and behind and around us. Now and then we came to small creeks, meadows, and a herdsman's ranch; but these were miles and miles apart, and hardly broke in on the sense of solitude. Early in the afternoon storms began to gather in the horizon. In straight columns the black clouds massed and journeyed; sometimes so swiftly that the eye had to move swiftly to follow them, and the spaces of sunlight and shadow on the sky seemed wheeling in circles; sometimes spreading slowly and blotting out a third of the horizon in gray mist. All the time we were in broad hot sun, looking out from our light into their darkness. We were nearing the western wall. As we came closer, we saw that there were myriads of lovely parks making up among the wooded foot-hills. These were the inlets of the old lake days; and of their rich soil had been born exquisite groves of aspen, lying now like solid mounds of green moss on the hill-sides. Toward sunset the storm columns thickened, blended, and swept down on all sides. Mountain after mountain and near hill after near hill were veiled in mist,—first white, then, gray, then dark blue-black. At last the last blue sky, the last clear spot surrendered. We were hemmed in completely in a great globe of rain. Drenched and dripping, but, for all that, glad of the rain—it had been such a masterly storm to see—we dashed on, turning northward and skirting the western hills, to the town of Fair Play. Fair Play is a mining town, one of the oldest in Colorado. It ought to be a beautiful village, lying as it does on a well-wooded slope at foot of grand mountains and on the Platte River. It is not. It is ill arranged, ill built, ill kept, dreary. Why cannot a mining town be clean, well-ordered, and homelike? I have never seen one such in Colorado or in California. Surely, it would seem that men getting gold first hand from Nature might have more heart and take more time to make home pleasant and healthful than men who earn their money by ordinary slow methods.

To enter Fair Play from the south, you go down into and up out of the Platte River. The Platte River just there is an odd place. It consists of, first, a small creek of water, then a sand-bar, then a pebble tract, then an iron pipe for mining purposes, then another pebble tract, then a wooden sluiceway for mining purposes, then a sand-bar with low aspen trees on it, then a second small stream of water, and lastly a pebble tract,—each side of these a frightful precipice. To go down the first precipice, across the creeks, sand-bars, pebble tracts, pipes, and sluiceways, and up the second precipice requires, for strangers new to the ways and blinded by gales of rain, some nerve. This was the way we entered Fair Play. We shall remember it.

At sunset the rain stopped; the clouds lifted and showed us the grand summit of Mount Lincoln, which we had come to ascend.

"Up to the top of that mountain in a carriage!" we exclaimed. "It is impossible."

"It is not even difficult," was the reply. "The road is as good a road as you have been over to-day. The steepness is the only trouble. It takes five hours to go from here, and it is only twelve miles to the summit."

We were incredulous. Mount Lincoln was nearly fifteen thousand feet high. It rose bare, precipitously, and seemed to pierce the sky. A bank of snow lay along its upper line.

"There's a mine just below that snowbank," continued the astonishing tale. "The miners live in a cabin there all the year round and there are loads of ore drawn down every day over this road you are going on."

The sides of the mountain looked more and more precipitous each moment that we gazed upon them. The story must be true, but it was incredible. The road must be real, but it was terrible to think of. We dreaded the morning. And it was the morning of a day which we would gladly live over again. So false are fears in this life.

We set out early,—down into the Platte meadows; up a rift between mountains, called a valley; along the edges of pine forests; past dismal little mining settlements, where great piles of sulphur smoked lurid and yellow,—seven miles of this, with the bare, brown, terrible mountains looming up straight and near before us, and we came to the base of Mount Lincoln. Seven miles we had come in a little more than an hour. It was to take us four hours to climb the remaining five miles. No wonder, at our first turn into the mountain road, we looked at each other aghast. It seemed nearly perpendicular. It was full of stones, of bowlders; it looked like the washed-out bed of a fierce mountain torrent. The pine forest on either hand was grand and stately. We could see no longer the bare summit above us; but, looking back, wc saw minute by minute, by the receding valley and the opening up of new views of hills and ravines and parks in all directions, how fast we were mounting. On all sides of us blazed enchanting color,—solid spaces of fire-weed, brilliant pink, purple and yellow and white asters, and blue hare-bells by tens of thousands; green grassy nooks under the pine trees were filled or bordered or dotted with the gay blossoms. The contrast between these and the devastated gully in which we were climbing seemed inexplicable. The horses' sides heaved like billows and their breathing was loud. Every two minutes they must stop to recover breath. Only the strongest brakes could hold the carriage in its place. "This is nothing," said Jack, the driver. "I don't mind anything about it below timber line."

Neither did we after we had been above timber line. That was some three thousand feet below the summit. Just there stood a group of cabins—the cabins and stables of the muleteers who work for the mines.

"You'll never get up with them hosses," called one of the mule-drivers, as we passed.

Jack received the taunt in contemptuous silence.

"I hain't never been by here yet without some o' them fellers tellin' me I couldn't get up," said he. "They think there can't nothin' go up this mountain except a mule."

"Well, when we come down all safe you can ask them which knew best," said I.

"No, I don't never say nothin' to 'em," replied Jack; "for as like as not some day I shan't get up, and then they'll fling it up at me. I'm the only fellow in our stable but what has had his hosses give out on this road."

We were out, fairly out on the bald, bare, blistering mountain,—on Mount Bross, which we must nearly cross to reach Mount Lincoln. The mountains, instead of being sheer solid rock, as we had supposed, looking at them from below, were simply piles, giant piles of fine-broken stone, broken into sharp, fine fragments, as if it had been crushed in a rolling mill,—not a single smooth roadstone among them, and so little sand or gravel or soil of any kind that it seemed a marvel how the great mass was held together; why strong winds did not blow it gradually away in showers of stones; why it was not perpetually rolling down; how it could possibly be tunnelled or driven over.

"There's the road," said Jack, pointing up to a dim zigzag line of a little lighter color than the rest of the mountain. "That's the worst place," indicating what looked like a track on which there had been a slide some day. "I shan't refuse anybody that likes to get out and walk there."

It was indeed fearful. Nothing but the grandeur of the off-look into space could have held our terror in check. That and the blue of the blue-bells all around us in great masses, making solid color as a cloverfield has. There they stood, the dainty, frail, beloved blue-bells, hugging the ground for safety; none of them more than three or four inches high, but clear, shining, and lovely as those which waved on the shady terraces below. Blue-bells twelve thousand feet above the sea, and they were not alone. There were dozens of other low flowers, which we knew not,—blue, white, lavender, and pink,—all keeping close to the ground, like mosses, but all perfect of form and tint. These comforted us. When for very dizziness we could not look up or off, we looked down to the ground, and there secure, content little faces reassured us.

The road wound and doubled, making occasional vertical thrusts upward. It seemed to have been made by pushing down the loose stones, bracing them and packing them a little tighter; that was all. Again and again we saw ahead of us what we supposed to be the road, and it proved to be only an accidental depression or projection in the mountain side. The horses could go only about twice or three times the carriage length at a time. Then, gasping and puffing, they stopped and rested five or six minutes. It seemed to me cruel to compel them to draw us. I jumped out and announced my intention of walking. A very few steps showed me that it was out of my power. Each step that I took seemed to resound in my head. I could not breathe. I was dizzy. My forehead seemed bursting from the pressure of the surging blood.

"Shade of Henry Bergh!" I exclaimed. "Couldst thou be humane at thirteen thousand feet above the sea? I cannot." And at the end of the first rod I called piteously to Jack that I must be taken into the carriage again. Two-thirds of the way up Mount Bross were several small cabins, projecting like odd-shaped rocks from the side of the mountain. Places for these also had apparently been scooped out among the fine rolling stones. This was the "Dolly Varden" Mine. Some of the miners stood in the cabin-doors as we passed. I gazed at them earnestly, expecting to see them look like sons of gnomes of the upper and lower air; but their faces were fresh, healthful, and kindly. A little further along Jack exclaimed:—

"We're riding over the Moose Mine now. There's tunnels right under us here that you could drive a four-hoss team through." Looking cautiously over the edge of the precipice to the right, we could see the roofs of the cabins many feet below us, and in a few moments we passed the road leading down to them. It was just such a road as we were on, and we could still see nothing but loose stone above, below, around. Mysterious mountain! Apparently a gigantic pile of tiny, rolling bits of stone, and yet mined and tunnelled and countertunnelled, and full of silver from top to bottom.

The road wound around the northern face of Mount Bross and then came out on a narrow ridge or saddle connecting Mount Bross to Mount Lincoln. This was perhaps the grandest point of all. To the north we looked up Mount Lincoln, a thousand feet above us; to the east we looked off and down to the river level, over and through and between myriads of sharp peaks and unfathomable gorges, and beyond these off to a horizon of mountains. To the west also we looked down into a confusion of peaks and ridges wedged between canyons; and just below us lay a small lake, so smooth, so dark it looked like a huge steel shield flung into the chasm.

As we ascended the last few hundred feet of Mount Lincoln a fierce wind blew in our faces. It seemed as if to such a wind it would be a trifling thing to whisk our carriage and us off the narrow ledge of road. Very welcome was the roaring fire in the cabin of the "Present Help" Mine at the summit, and very significant seemed the name of the mine.

Nothing in the mining country is odder than the names of the mines. They are as indicative of parentage as are the names of men and women; and, overhearing them in familiar conversations, one is often much bewildered. Once on a hotel piazza I overheard the following sentences:—

"He's sold out i' the Moore and bought into the Moskeeter; 'n he's got suthin' in Hiawatha, too."

"Well, I think Buckskin Joe's pretty good, don't you?" replied the listener.

The cabin was, like those of the Dolly Vardin Mine, below, built against the side of the mountain, in a spot apparently scooped out of the stones. From its front was a transcendent off-look to the south and east. Its door was perhaps three feet from the edge of a sheer precipice. Hundreds and, for aught I know, thousands of feet down would that man fall who made a misstep; and yet the men went back and forth swiftly, and jostled the mules carelessly to one side if they happened to wander in there. We, however, crept slowly around the cabin corner, holding by the logs, and did not venture to look off until we were fairly in the doorway.

The cook was a cheery fellow, with a fine head and laughing brown eyes. He was kneading bread. His tin pans shone like a dairymaid's. The cabin was by no means a comfortless place. One wide, long bench for table; a narrow one for chairs; tin cups, tin pans, black knives and forks,—we borrowed them all. The cook made delicious coffee for us and we took our lunch with as good relish as if we had been born miners. The men's beds were in tiers of bunks on two sides of the cabin, much wider and more comfortable than state room berths in steamers. In each berth was a small wooden box, nailed on the wall, for a sort of cupboard or bureau drawer. In these lay the Sunday clothes, white shirts, and so forth, neatly folded. There were newspapers lying about, and when I asked the cook if he liked living there, he answered: "Oh, yes! very well. We have a mail once a week." A reply which at once revealed the man and was significant of the age in which he lived.

There were still two hundred feet of Mount Lincoln to be climbed. The little cabin had seemed to be but a step below the summit-line; but now we looked up to two sharp pyramids of stones above us. Up to the first point, over fine, sharp bits of stone, which slipped and rolled under our feet at every step, we crawled; up to the second, over great bowlders, piled and poised and tipped on each other, we scrambled and leaped, and sunk down at the foot of the flagstaff. We were literally on the apex point of the continent! Here, on the one hand, were the head-waters of the Arkansas River, going south; on the other, the head-waters of the Platte, going east; and just across a small divide, almost within a stone's throw, the head-waters of the Grande, going west to the Pacific. Well did the old Spaniards name this central range "Sierra Madre"—"Mother Mountains." It is said that the view from this peak has a radius of over a hundred and fifty miles. It would be easy to believe it greater. Fancy such a radius as this sweeping slowly around a horizon circle of lofty peaks, and the entire space from the outer horizon to the central summit filled with great mountain ranges and their intervening parks and valleys. The great South Park, a day's journey wide, was a hand's-breadth now of soft olive-gray, its wooded ridges and hills making dots of dark color; yet its tint and its outline were as distinct as when seen from its near wall.

As we looked down on the narrow chains and into the closer chasms, it seemed as if this great giant pyramid on which we stood must hold, in some mysterious way, in its secret chambers, the threads of all the other ranges, as if they centred in it, radiated out from it, circled around it, in an intricate bond, like that by which the spider-web is spun and swung. The near peaks and ridges were bare, stony, sharp. Their chasms looked unfathomable, like ghastly seams cloven to the earth's very centre. Among these, to the north, were two silent, black, gleaming lakes. From these nearer peaks the eye journeyed downward, with a sense of relief, to wooded ranges, intervals of sunny valley; and then outward, in the vast circle, to mountains with snowy tops; and at last to mountains in the furthest horizon, blue, dim, and unreal,— mountains of which one could unquestioningly believe that they were not of this world, but of some other,—parapets of some far planet, on which at that moment beings of an unknown race might be standing and looking off across the great space wondering at us.

Who knows that among the "things prepared" there may not be this: that, we being set free from all hindrances of space, as well as from those of time, there will be recognition, converse from planet to planet, the universe round as quick and complete as there is now from face to face within hand's reach. On such heights as this one sees clearly, and feels a million times more clearly than he sees, that this glorious world could never have been fashioned solely for the uses of our present helplessness. Deeper than the secret stores of gold and silver and gems with which these great untouched mountains are filled, there lies in them a secret, a prophecy of life to come, into which they shall enter and of which we shall be triumphant possessors.

With brakes clinched, wheels tied, and teeth set, we grazed, twisted, slid down the mountain; none too soon, for a storm was gathering in the west, which gave us a hard race down the valley and across the river meadows. But we came in ahead at sunset, and were warming our hands over a big fire in the Fair Play Hotel when it burst in avalanches of cold rain.

"This is snow on the mountains," said the landlord. Sure enough. Next morning all the upper peaks were solid white,— so white that it was hard to see where snow left off and clouds began. As we looked back and up from the bed of the Platte at the majestic shining pyramids and cones, we doubted our memories of the day before. As well tell us we had been caught up into the skies.

We were a very glad party that morning. We were setting our faces toward an unanticipated pleasure; more than that, toward a pleasure we had longed for but had unwillingly abandoned all hope of. We were setting out for the Twin Lakes. We owed this to Jack. Jack was a reticent fellow. A hasty observer might have thought his face a sullen one; but there were fine lines around the corners of his eyes which showed a sensitive nature. He had led a wild life. He had been a stage-driver in Mexico; had spent whole winters trapping on the shores of Itaska Lake; had fought Indians everywhere; and just now was lying by in inglorious quiet in a Fair Play livery stable. Before he had been long with us on the mountain, he knew what we liked. The first remark which betrayed his discriminating observation was called out by our enthusiastic ejaculations about the flowers. Without turning his head and speaking low, as if in a soliloquy, he said: "There's great differences in folks about noticin' things."

Have we the tutor of Sandford and Merton for a driver? thought I, and I smothered a laugh as I said: "Yes, indeed, Jack. But what reminded you of that?"

"I was a-thinkin' of the two people I drove up here day before yesterday. I never heard 'em say one word from first to last about any thin' they see' an' they wanted to turn right an' come straight down 's soon 's they got up. I don't know what such folks 's them takes the trouble to travel round for. I s'pose it's just for the name on't— to say they've done it."

The words give no idea of the drollery and contemptuousness of his manner. We could hardly reply for laughing.

"Oh! Jack, didn't they even notice the flowers?" we said.

"Don't believe they'd have said there was a flower on the road," replied Jack. "All they see was the stones and the steep places. The man, he swore at 'em."

"But there ain't nothin' that you'll see to-day," he continued, "which is 's handsome, to my way o' thinkin', 's the Twin Lakes. You're goin' there, ain't you?"

"No, Jack," we said. "We can't take the time to go there." Jack's countenance fell.

"Can't you?" he said. "I'd like first-rate to have you see them lakes. They're the nicest things in this country." Again and again in the course of the day he alluded to them. It evidently went sorely against him that we should not see those lakes.

"You like flowers so much," he said. "You hain't seen any flowers yet to what you'll see there, an' there ain't no kind of difficulty in gettin' to the Twin Lakes. It's a plain road from Fair Play."

"Yes, Jack," we said; "but it is two days' journey, and we can't spend so much time."

Jack fairly sprang round on his seat, and, facing us, exclaimed:—

"Who's been a-tellin' you it was two days' journey? It's only thirty-five miles straight across the range. You'll do it easy in one day."

And so, all by reason of Jack's having noticed the "differences in people about noticin' things," we set off on the fourth morning of our Holy Week for the Twin Lakes.

"Jack," said I, as we were climbing up out of the Platte River, "what is the reason you like the Twin Lakes so much?"

An awkward, half-shamefaced look flickered over Jack's features, as if I had asked him some question about his sweetheart.

"I don't know," he said, hesitatingly. "I reckon it's because it's such a lonely-lookin' kind o'place. I hain't been there but once."

There was a strange mixture of the hermit and the adventurer in our Jack. We liked journeying in his company.

We were out once more in the great, grand South Park. It was glorious under the morning light. Its broad stretches shone silver-gray, and its myriad-mountained wall was blue in the south and in the east and in the west snow-topped. We drove a few miles southward, then turned sharply to the west, and followed a grassy road into one of the many lovely valleys which we had seen two days before, making up like inlets between the foot-hills of the western wall of the Park. This wall we were to cross. Its multiplying and towering crests looked impassable; but we had learned the marvel of the secret windings of mountain passes, and a messenger had already met us,—a messenger white with haste, so fast had he come down and out.

By the same road we would go up and in, and so across. Almost immediately the valley narrowed. The creek, the messenger, became a foaming brook and the road clung to its bank. It was thick set with willows, bush-maples, and alders. Their branches brushed into our faces, they grew so close; flowers burst into our sight like magic on all sides,— fireweed, harebells, painter's-brush, larkspur, asters of all colors and superbly full and large. It was a fairy garden. The grass was green,—real, perfect green grass, the first, the only true green grass I have ever seen in Colorado. Except for the towering and stony walls above our heads and for the fiery scarlet of the painter's-brush and the tall spikes of larkspur, I could have fancied myself in a wild thicketed cave in Vermont. The green grass ran up in lovely spaces under the pines and firs; the air was almost overladen with fragrance; white butterflies wheeled and circled above us and then flew on ahead; the road was set, literally set, thick with borders of lavender, gray, purple, white, and yellow asters. Even down the middle of the road they grew,—not only asters, but harebells; under the horses' feet, safe, untouched, in the narrow central strip of grass, lifted high between the two trodden furrows.

The rocky walls narrowed and still narrowed; we were at bottom of a chasm. Then imperceptibly our road would rise, its borders widen, and we would find ourselves on a narrow divide, with deep ravines on either hand. I am at utter loss to describe how these Rocky Mountain ridges underlie, overlie, cross, and swallow up each other. They remind me of nothing but masses of colossal crystals, so sharp their edges, so straight their sides, so endless their intersections. They are gigantic wedges driven into the mountains and each other, and piled up again in tiers, making mountains upon mountains. The ravines between them seen to have been cloven by them, as an axe cleaves wood and remains fast in the rift it has made.

Over and on and up and down these wedged ridges, through unvarying pine and fir forests and through ever-varying flower-beds, we slowly climbed the range. At last the pines and firs stopped. We were eleven thousand feet high. The bare ridge on which we were, tapered to a point before us and disappeared in the side of a stony peak. A small dark lake lay in the hollow just below their intersection. A sharp wind blew from the left; we were at the top. We looked over into another ravine. A dark wooded mountain shut across it like a gate; between us and it were a bit of meadow and a little stream.

After these, the ravine narrowed again and the road grew steep and rocky,—very steep and very rocky. Through a very carnival of bowlders, fallen pines, driftwood, and foaming water we descended. Soon, through a grand rock gateway, we saw the valley of the Arkansas, olive-gray, with meandering lines of solid green marking the river course, and with strange and exquisitely beautiful terraces in it, rising abruptly and in detached curves,—the record of changing water-lines in the ancient days. As we reached the edge of the valley, we saw a faint track leading off to the left.

"Ah!" said Jack. "Here's the short cut." And he turned into it.

"What short cut?" said I, being by nature and by experience distrustful of short cuts to any thing.

"There's a short cut through here down to the river, that saves four miles. So McLaughlin said. He's been through here. It don't look much work, though; that's a fact," said Jack, as we drove into the meadow grass.

Zigzagging around that meadow, now in now out of sight, over boggy places and round hillocks, led that "short cut." We were in no danger of losing our way, for there lay the Arkansas meadows in full sight; but the road seemed to be making no special headway toward them. The question was about the ford. Should we hit it? Presently we came out into a travelled road and in full sight of the Arkansas River; that is, of several tortuous lines of alders and willows in a bright green meadow. Not a gleam of water to be seen. Neither did our short cut in any wise cross this travelled road, which ran parallel with the river. There was no suggestion of track leading down to the river at this point. Slowly we drove up and down that road, peering into the grass on its river side for sign or trail of a road leading to a ford. There was none. At last, Jack, giving the horses a revengeful stroke, as if they had suggested the short cut, poor things! drove rapidly up the road, saying: "Well, I reckon we'll save time to drive up to the ford I know, four miles up the road."

"So much for short cuts, Jack. They never turn out well," said I, as we passed the point where the road we had forsaken joined the one we were on. It would have brought us to the ford an hour sooner.

After the ford, six miles down-stream again, through the luscious meadow grass, in which cows grazed ankle-deep. The mountains we had crossed stood bare and red in the east, the mountains we were still to enter stood soft and blue in the west,—two high ranges, and the Arkansas River and its meadows between; and yet we were in that very world of near peaks and ravines and ridges upon which we had looked down from Mount Lincoln the day before. We had thought it all mountains. Yet here in one of those chasms, which had looked to us like nothing more than clefts, there was room for a river, and river meadows, homesteads, and herds.

The sun was so low that he cast huge profiles of shadow on all the northern slopes of the western mountains, as we turned toward them. Once more to the right, once more into a grassy valley making up between the foot-hills; soft, round, covered only with low grass and a pale bluish shrub, they fairly shimmered in their ghostly gray as the twilight settled on them. One, two, three, four, five we climbed, and seemed to get no nearer the mountains. "I'd forgotten there were so many of these hills," said Jack. But we did not; nor after the next, nor the next. At last the sight came,—beautiful enough to have been waited for. Before us a line of high, sharp peaks, dark blue nearly to the top, their summits just touched by the red sunset-light. They seemed to curve westward and to curve eastward till they met the terraced line of hills on which we stood. At their feet and at ours lay the two lakes,—dark, motionless, shining, stretching close to the mountain bases on all sides, and linked to each other by a narrow neck of green land, across which a line of green bushes stretched, looking like a second band set to strengthen or to adorn the first. Afterward we saw that it was a closer link than we dreamed; for beneath the line of green bushes runs a little creek, mingling the waters of the upper and the lower lake perpetually.

Jack turned and looked at us in silence.

"Yes, you were right, Jack," we said. "It is more beautiful than anything we saw yesterday, and it is a very lonely-looking kind of place."

Not so lonely as we could have wished, however, when we drove down the steep hills to the Log Cabin Hotel, where we must sleep. People walking about, white-covered camp-wagons, high-topped buggies, all told us that we were too late on the list of arrivals.

"Indeed, I can't,—not to make you anyways comfortable," was the landlady's honest answer when we appeared at her door, saying: "Here we four are, and must stay. Can you take care of us?" It wasn't so bad as it might have been, that wind-swept, fluttering room in which we went to bed that night, bounded to west by a chinky log wall, to north by an open window, to east and south by a scant calico curtain, which parted, but did not sever us from the dining-room. Colorado travellers have often fared worse, no doubt; but, taking all things into account, we thought it an odd coincidence that over at the head of one very unrestful bed there should have been pasted a leaf of "The Overland Monthly," containing the first stanzas of an "Ode to Pain." Never shall I cease to regret that we were so stupefied by lack of sleep and by the repeated alarms at the fluttering calico curtain that we omitted to copy that "Ode to Pain." The pattern of the calico of the calico curtain I recollect perfectly,—it is stamped on my brain forever; but not a line of the Ode can I recall.

All the next morning we sat under a pine-tree on the northern shore of the lakes and looked out upon them. Marvellous, lovely twins! Ten thousand feet above the sea and thousands of miles away from it, they held all its charm and none of its sadness. The soft waves lapped on the shore with a sound as gentle as the sigh of pines, and the water was clear as crystal sixty feet down. They were seas, translated, glorified, come to their spiritual resurrection, and wedded to each other for all eternity. The lower lake is about three miles in length; the upper one only half as long. They are not more than a mile and a half wide. But when you sit on the shore, and see the great mountains' full height and reaching only half way across, they seem much wider. The mountains are wooded half way up. The green line of firs and pines and aspens reproduces on the mountain side exactly the line which the summits make against the sky. This beautiful, jagged summit line, therefore, is three times mapped in the beautiful picture,—mapped first in red against the blue sky, then in green on the mountain side, and then red and green outlines both are mapped again together on the dark amber of the lake. The picture seemed to be drawn by a trembling hand. At the slightest breeze on the surface it quivered and was effaced, but returned in an instant again if the breeze died down. As we drove away in the early afternoon, along the terraced hills on the northern shore, the lakes were motionless, and dark blue as tempered steel, and the picture of the wooded mountains stretched across the shining surface in lines as fine and distinct as Damascus ever graved on her magic metal for blade or shield.

We followed the lake outlet down toward the Arkansas meadows again, over more of the soft, sage-gray hills, past deserted mining villages where grass grew high round blackened hearthstones, and past villages where men are still mining for gold, down, down as fast as the creek into the fertile bottom-lands. The Arkansas here is narrow, and doubles on itself perpetually, as if it sought to baffle some pursuer. Its meadow at this point is a delicious bit of color. First the curving lines of willows and cottonwoods, dark green; then the rank meadow grass, bright yellow-green; then the foothill slopes of the exquisite gray-green, paling to silver-gray at top, and with the red soil gleaming through everywhere; then the dark, wooded slopes of the mountains, reaching up to ten or eleven thousand feet, and above those the bare peaks, gray, or red, or blue, or purple, according to the day and the hour. Again and again I wonder at the ineffable loveliness of the soft tints in this stem-visaged country. Again and again I long for an artist to come who can seize the secret of their tenderness, the bloom of their beauty. The meadow grew less and less,—from fields to narrow strips, from strips to fringes it diminished, and the mountains came closer and closer. On every side of us were weird and fantastic rocks, shaped in all manner of semblances, so distorted, so uncouth, so significant of ages of violence, that they were almost fearful. At sunset we looked out to the mouth of this canyon on a scene bewilderingly beautiful. No mirage in the desert ever played a more fantastic trick upon traveller's eyes than did the sweet light and mist slanting over the distance beyond the mouth of the canyon. Against the southern sky rose one of the highest mountain ranges, its summit-line majestically cut into square buttress shapes in the centre, and in slowly lowering peaks, and undulations to right and left. It was two-thirds in shadow,—deep, dark blue,—the upper third so bathed in light that the clouds floating above it seemed part of it, and we disputed with each other hotly as to where the real crests of the mountain were. At foot of this range, bathed in a golden light and yet misty and pale blue in parts, there lay what seemed to be a great city of Oriental architecture. Domes and minarets and towers and roofs,—nothing could be plainer. The light streamed in among them; the beams lay in dusty gold aslant across them; shining spots here and there looked like the kindling reflections of sunlight on glass surfaces. What could it be? No city, certainly. It was into the wilderness we gazed, but what did the shapes mean? They were far too solid to be mere atmospheric effects, optical illusions. As well as if we were touching their foundations, we knew that they were solid, real. Behind us the western sky was one sheet of gold. Floating crimson clouds hung low over the near mountains, and the east was clear blue. Slowly the city sank into shadow. Even after it was wrapped in gray, the domes and the minarets and the towers remained. It was a city still. And we drove down into the valley almost believing that some strange chance had brought us to that height at the exact moment when the sun's rays had revealed some unknown ruins in a hollow of the great hills.

There could hardly be a sharper contrast than that from the gorgeous color and fairy-like spectacle on which we had been feasting at top of the hill, to the dank, dark hollow into which a few moments brought us;—to the low, flat-roofed cabins, and the sad, worn face of the woman who stood in their doorway.

The cabins were built close to the bank of the river. Hills to the north and to the south shut in all the dampness and shut out hoursful of sun. There was a heavy and ill-odored moisture in the air, such as I had not supposed could exist in Colorado. I shuddered at the thought that we must sleep in it.

In reply to the question whether she could take care of us for the night, the sad-faced woman answered:—

"I'll do the best I can."

The expression of her face made my heart ache. She looked ill, hopeless; every feature showed refinement, and her voice and her words were those of an educated woman.

"I am sure you are from the East," I said to her. The tears filled her eyes instantly.

"Yes, I am from New York State," she said, and turned away.

Before night we knew her whole story. It seemed to be a relief to her to tell it to us. She had been a school teacher in western New York. Of delicate fibre physically, and of an unusually fine and sensitive mental organization, she was as unfitted for life in the Colorado wildernesses as a woman could well be. Yet she had borne up under bravely until the last three years, when ill health had been added to her other burdens. Within the last month, two of her three children had died, and this last blow had broken her heart. One had died of scarlet fever, and the other, she said, "of this dreadful new disease that the doctors don't know much about,—the cerebro-spinal meningitis, they call it, or some such name."

Poor babies! No wonder, living in that damp hollow, with the river miasms, if there were any, shut in and kept over from night to night in the low-roofed cabin!

The remaining child, a little boy of six or eight, looked very pale and lifeless. He too had the fever. It would have seemed cruel to say to that helpless mother, "The only chance for healthful life for him and for you is a new house on some sunny hillside." Yet I yearned to say it. It will be long before I forget that sad little home on the Arkansas.

The next morning—our sixth morning—we set out early on our homeward way. A few miles brought us to the magic city of the night before. The marvel was not so strange. Here were hills, upon hills,—sharp, rounded, crowded, piled with rocks, which even by day bore almost the shapes they had shown to us by night,—pinnacles, buttresses, terraces, towers, with sharp-pointed firs growing among them. It was indeed a city—a silent, tenantless city—which reminded me of some of the stories I read in my childhood of Edom and Petraea. We were in the canyon still, but it was fast widening and bearing to the right. The way of the Arkansas River lay south, and we could follow it no longer. We must turn northward and climb the range again. We had lost many hundred feet of elevation in coming down this easier way by the river's road. Five hours of good climbing did it. Over divide after divide, as we had so many times climbed before; under the pines and among the flowers and out on the bare ridges at top; then down, miles down, into the grand, steadfast, reposeful plain of the park. We were a half day's journey now to the south of Fair Play and our road skirted the western wall of the park. We looked up into all the lovely valleys, thrusting their arms into the forest slopes of the mountains. They were alike and not alike,—all green and smooth and creek-fed, but no two of the same outline, no two of the same depth, any more than any two of the inlets on a fretted seashore. A night at Fair Play again, and then we retraced our road of the first two days,—eastward, instead of westward, across the park; eastward over the mountains and through the passes, and at sunset of the eighth day down into our own beloved plains. The first glimpse of their immeasurable distance was grander than all we had journeyed to see.

Their mystic vanishing line, where earth and sky seem one, only because eyes are too weak to longer follow their eternal curves, always strikes upon my sight as I think there would fall upon the ear the opening perfect chord of some celestial symphony,—a celestial symphony which we must forever strain to hear, must forever know to be resounding just beyond our sense, luring our very souls out of this life into the next, from earth to heaven.

Only, as I said, from a Saturday to a Saturday. But what a week it had been,—the Holy Week of our summer!

Our New Road

Of all the mountains in Colorado, Jackson's favorite was Cheyenne Mountain. In "Our New Road," she explained why she loved this mountain so dearly. She also included in this essay a vivid description of her favorite mountain plant, the kinnikinnick. "Our New Road" was first published in the December 1876 issue of ATLANTIC MONTHLY under the title "A Colorado Road."

What a new singer or a new play is to the city man, a new road is to the man of the wilderness. I fancy the parallel might be drawn out and amplified, much to the exaltation of the new road, if the man of the wilderness chose to boast, and if people were sensible enough to value pleasures as they do other fabrics, by their wear. It would be cruel, however, to make the city man discontented. Poor fellow! he is joined to his idols of stone, buried alive above them now, and soon he will be buried dead below them. Let him alone! It is no part of my purpose in this paper to enter the lists in defence of my joys, or to make an attack upon his. It is merely to describe our new road; and my pronoun "our" is by no means a narrow one,—it is a big plural, taking in some four thousand souls, all the dwellers in the town of Colorado Springs and its near neighborhood.

The "new road" is up and across Cheyenne Mountain. Cheyenne Mountain is the southernmost peak of the grand range which lies six miles west of our town. Only those who dwell at the feet of great mountain ranges know how like a wall they look, what sense of fortified security they give; people who come for a day, to gaze and pass by, or even people who stay and paint the hills' portraits, know very little. A mountain has as much personality as a man; you do not know one any more than you know the other until

you have summered and wintered him. You love one, and are pro-
foundly indifferent to another, just as it is with your feeling towards
your neighbors; and it is often as hard to give good and sufficient
reason for your preference in the one case as in the other. But no
lover of Cheyenne was ever at loss to give reasons for his love. The
mountain is so unique in its grandeur and dignity that one must be
blind and stolid indeed not to feel its influence.

As I said, it is the southernmost peak of the range lying west
of Colorado Springs. This is as if I said it is the southern bastion of
our western wall. It is only two or three thousand feet above the
town (the town be it remembered, lies six thousand feet above the
sea). Pike's Peak, a few miles farther north, in the same range, is
nearly twice as high; so it is not by reason of height that Cheyenne
is so grand. Pausing now, with my pen in my hand, I look out of
my south window at its majestic front, and despair of being loyal to
the truth I would like to tell of this mountain. Is it that its eastern
outline, from the summit down to the plain, is one slow, steady, in-
curving slope, broken only by two rises of dark timber-lands, which
round like billows; and that this exquisite hollowing curve is for
ever outlined against the southern sky: Is it that the heavily cut and
jagged top joins this eastern slope at a sharp angle, and stretches away
to the northwest in broken lines as rugged and strong as the eastern
slope is graceful and harmonious; and that the two lines together
make a perpetual, vast triangulation on the sky? Is it that when white
clouds in our heavens at noon journey south, they always seem to
catch on its eastern slope, and hang and flutter there, or nestle
down in an island-like bank reaching half-way up the mountain? Is
it that the dawn always strikes it some moments earlier than it
reaches the rest of the range, turning it glowing red from plains to
sky, like a great illumined cathedral? Is it that the setting sun also
loves it, and flings back mysterious broken prisms of light on its furrowed western slopes, long after the other peaks are black and grim?
Is it that it holds canyons where one can climb, among fir-trees and
roses and clematis and columbine and blue-bells and ferns and

mosses, to wild pools and cascades in which snow-fed brooks tumble and leap? These questions are only like the random answers of one suddenly hard pressed for the explanation of a mystery which has long since ceased to be a mystery to him,—ceased to be a mystery not because it has been fathomed, but because it has become familiar and dear. No lover of Cheyenne but will say that Cheyenne is better than all these; that no one of all these is quite truly and sufficiently told; and I myself in the telling feel like one stammering in a language but half learned, the great mountain all the while looking down on me in serene and compassionate silence. At this moment, it looks like a gigantic mountain of crystals, purple and white. Every smallest ridge slope fronting to the east or south is of a red purple, like the purple of a Catawba grape over-ripe; every smallest ridge slope to the north or west is white like the white of alabaster, and soft with the softness of snow. The plains are a clear, pale yellow, and the spot where the slope melts into the level, and the purpose melts into the yellow, is a triumph of shape and color from which men who paint might well turn away sorrowful.

Knowing well, as I do, just where among these crystalline ridges our new road winds, I yet look up incredulous at the sharp precipices and ledges. But it is there, bless it!—our new uplifter, revealer, healer, nearer link of approach to a nearer sky! The workmen know it as the road over to Bear creek valley, and they think they have built it for purposes of traffic, and for bringing down railroad ties; it is a toll-road, and the toll-gatherer takes minute reckoning of all he can see passing his door. But I think there will always be a traffic which the workmen will not suspect, and a viewless company which will elude the toll-gatherer, on this new road of ours.

It was on one of our tropical midwinter days that I first climbed it. A mile southward from the town, then a sharp turn to the west, fronting the mountains as directly as if our road must be going to pierce their sides, across brooks where the ice was so thick that our horses' hoofs and our wheels crunched slowly through, up steep banks on which there were frozen glares of solid ice, and across open levels where the thin snow lay in a fine tracery around every separate grassstalk,—one, two, three miles of this, and we were at the base of the mountain, and saw the new road, a faint brown track winding up the yellow slope and disappearing among the pines.

As we turned into the road, we saw, on our right, two ranchmen leaning, in the Sunday attitude, against a fence, and smoking. As we passed, one of them took his pipe from his mouth and said nonchalantly, "S'pose ye *know* this ere's a toll-road." The emphasis on the word "know" conveyed so much that we laughed in his face. Clever monosyllable, it stood for a whole paragraph.

"Oh, yes," we said, "we know it. It's worth fifty cents, isn't it, to get high up on Cheyenne Mountain?"

"Well, yes," he replied, reflectively, "'spose 'tis. It's a mighty good road, anyhow. Found blossom rock up there yesterday," he added, with the odd, furtive, gleaming expression which I have so often seen in the eyes of men who spoke of a possible or probable mine; "true blossom rock. The assayer, he was up, an he says it's the real mineral, no mistake," he continued, and there seemed a fine and unconscious scorn in the way he fingered the dingy and torn paper half dollar with which we had paid for the right to drive over what might be chambers of silver and gold.

"Blossom rock," I said, "why 'blossom'?" To call this particular surface mineral the flower of the silver root lying below, is a strange fancy, surely; it seems a needlessly poverty stricken device for Nature's realms to borrow names from each other.

A few rods' steep climb, and we have left the foot-hill and are absolutely on the mountain. The road tacks as sharply as a ship in a gale; we are facing north instead of south, and are already on a ledge so high that we have a sense of looking over as well as of looking off. The plains have even now the pale pink flush which only distance gives, and our town, though it is only four miles away, looks already like a handful of yellow and white pebbles on a sand beach, so suddenly and so high are we lifted above it. We are not only on the mountain, we are among the rocks,—towering rocks of bright red sandstone, thick-grown in spaces with vivid yellow-green lichen. They are almost terrible, in spite of their beauty of color,—so high, so straight, so many-pointed are they. The curves of the road would seem to be more properly called loops, so narrow are they, so closely do they hug the sharp projections round which they turn and wind and turn and wind. One is tempted to say that the road has lassoed the mountain and caught it, like a conquered Titan, in a tangle of coils. At every inner angle of the curves is a wide turn-out, where we wait to give the horses breath, and to watch if there be any one coming down. Round the outer angles we go at a slow pace, praying that there may be no one just the other side. When we face northward, the mountain shuts off all sun and we are in cold shadow; the instant we double the outer point of the ridge and face southward, we are in full sunshine; thus we alternate from twilight to high noon, and from high noon to twilight, in a swift and bewildering succession. On our right, we look down into chasms bristling with sharp rocks and pointed tops of fir-trees; on our left the mountain-side rises, now abruptly like a wall, now in sloping tiers. After a mile of these steep ascents, we come out on a very promontory of precipices. Here we turn the flank of the mountain, and a great vista to the west and north opens up before us, peak rising above peak, with softer hills crowding in between; below us, canyon after canyon, ridge after ridge, a perfect net-work of ins and outs and ups and downs, and our little brown thread of a road swinging along at easy levels above it all. There is no more hard climbing. There are even down slopes on which the horses trot, in the shade of high pine-trees on either hand, now and then coming upon a spot where the ridge has widened sufficiently for the trees to dispose themselves in a more leisurely and assured fashion, like a lowland grove, instead of clinging at a slant on steep sides, as they are for the most part driven to do; now and then coming out on opens, where a canyon lies bare and yawning, like a great gash in the mountain's side, its slopes of fine red or yellow gravelly sand seeming to be in a perpetual slide from top to bottom,—only held

Helen Hunt Jackson's Trip to South Park and the
Upper Arkansas ("Our New Road"), 1875

Present Highways 285 and 24 for reference only

in place by bowlders here and there, which stick out like grotesque heads of rivets with which the hill had been mended. Here we find the kinnikinnick in its perfection, enormous mats of it lying compact, glossy, green and claret-tinted, as if enamelled, on the yellow sand. Painters have thought it worth while to paint over and over again some rare face or spot whose beauty perpetually eluded their grasp and refused to be transferred to canvas. Why should I not be equally patient and loyal to this exquisite vine, of which I have again and again, and always vainly, tried to say what it is like, and how beautiful is the mantle it flings over bare and stony places?

Imagine that a garden-border of box should lay itself down and behave like a blackberry vine,—run, and scramble, and overlap, and send myriads of long tendrils out in all directions,—and you have a picture of the shape, the set of the leaf, the thick matting of the branches, and the utter unrestrainedness of a root of kinnikinnick. Add to this the shine of the leaf of the myrtle, the green of green grass in June, and the claret-red of the blackberry vine in November, and you will have a picture of its lustrousness and its colors. The solid centres of the mats are green; the young tendrils run out more and more vivid red to their tips. In June it is fragrant with clusters of small pink and white bells, much like the huckleberry blossom. In December it is gay with berries as red as the berries of the holly. Neither midsummer heat nor midwinter cold can tarnish the sheen nor shrivel the fulness of its leaf. It has such vitality that no barrenness, no drought, deters it; in fact, it is more luxuriant on the bare, gravelly slopes of which I was just now speaking, than I have ever seen it elsewhere. Yet its roots seem to take slight hold of the soil. You may easily, by a little care in loosening the tendrils, pull up solid mats five to seven feet long. Fancy these at Christmas, in one's house. I look up, as I write, at one upon my own wall. It has a stem an inch in diameter, gnarled and twisted like an old cedar,—the delight of an artistic eye, the surprise and scorn of the Philistine, to whom it looks merely like fire-wood. From this gnarled bough bursts a great growth of luxuriant green branches, each branch claret-red at its tips and vivid green at its centre. It has hung as a crown of late dower over the head of my Beatrice Cenci for two months, and not a leaf has fallen. It will hang there unchanged until June, if I choose. This virtue is partly its own, partly the spell of the wonderful dryness of our Colorado air, in which all things do as Mrs. Stowe says New Englanders do when they are old,—"dry up a little and then last."

Still running westward along the north side of the mountain, the road follows the ridge lines of the huge, furrow-like canyons which cleave the mountain from its base to its summit. These make a series of triangles piercing the solid mass; and we zigzag up one side, round the sharp inner corner, and down the other side, round the outer point, and then up and down just such another triangle,—and so on, for miles. The sight of these great gorges is grand: a thousand feet down to their bottom on the one hand, and a thousand feet up to their top on the other. Looking forward or back across them, we see the line of our road like a narrow ledge on the precipice; a carriage on it looks as if it had been let down by ropes from the top. Soon we come to great tracts of pines and firs, growing scantily at incredible angles on these steep slopes; many trees have been cut, and are lying about on the ground, as if giants had been playing jackstraws, and had gone away leaving their game unfinished. They call these trees "timber;" that is "corpse" for a tree. A reverent sadness always steals on my thoughts when I see a dead tree lying where the axe slew it. The road winds farther and farther into a labyrinth of mountain fastnesses; gradually these become clear to the eye, a certain order and system in their succession. The great Cheyenne Canyon stretches like a partially hewn pathway between the mountain we are on and the rest of the range lying to the north of it. This northward wall is rocky, seamed, and furrowed; bare, water-worn cliffs, hundreds of feet high, alternate with intervals of pine forest, which look black and solid in the shade, but in full sunlight are seen to be sparse, so that even from the other side of the canyon you may watch every tree's double of black shadow thrown on the ground below, making a great rafter-work floor, as it were, from which the trees seem to rise like columns. Above this stretch away endless tiers of peaks and round hills, more than one can count, because at each step some of them sink out of sight and new ones crop up. Some are snow-topped; some have a dark, serrated line of firs over their summits; some look like mere masses of bowlders and crags, their upper lines standing clear out against the sky, like the jagged top of a ruined wall. On all the slopes leading down into the canyons are rows of pines, like besiegers climbing up; and on most of the upper connecting ridges lies a fine white line of snow, like a silver thread knitting peak to peak. From all the outer points of these gorges, as we look back to the east, we have exquisite glimpses of the plains, framed always in a triangle made by sloping canyon walls. I doubt if it would be possible to render one of these triangle pictures as we get them from between these intersecting and overlapping walls. A yucca plant, ten inches high, may happen to come into the near foreground, so that it helps to frame them; and yet their upper horizon line is miles and miles away. I have never seen so marvellous a blending of the far and the near as they give.

Still the road winds and winds, and the sense of remoteness grows stronger and stronger. The silence of the wilderness, what is there like it? The silence of the loneliest ruin is silence only because time has hushed the sounds with which the ruin was once alive. This is silence like that in which the world lay pregnant before time again.

Just as this grand, significant silence was beginning to make us silent, too, we came suddenly upon a little open where the wilderness was wilderness no longer. One man had tamed it. On our right hand stood his forge, on our left his house. Both forge and house were of a novel sort; nowhere but in the heart of the Rocky Mountains would they have been called by such names. The forge consisted of a small pine-tree, a slender post some four feet distant from it, a pile of stones and gravel, a log, and a pair of bellows. The house was perhaps eight feet high; the walls reached up one third that height:

first, three logs, then, two planks; there the wall ended. One front post was a pine-tree, the other a rough cedar stump; from the ridge-pole hung a sail-cloth roof which did not meet the walls; very airy must be the blacksmith's house on a cold night, in spite of the southeast winds being kept off by a huge bowlder twenty feet high. On one side stood an old dead cedar-tree with crooked arms, like some marine monster; one of the arms was the blacksmith's pantry, and there hung his dinners for a week or more, a big haunch of venison. A tomtit, not much larger than a humming-bird, was feasting on it by snatches. The tiny creature flew from the topmost branch of the tree down to the venison, took a bite, and was back again safe on the upper bough in far less time than I take to write his name; less than a second a trip he took, I think; never once did he pause for a second bite, never once rest on a lower branch: he fairly seemed to buzz in the air, so fast he flew up and down.

"So you board the tomtit, do you?" we said to the blacksmith, who stood near by, piling boughs on a big fire.

"Yes; he's so little I can afford to keep him," replied the black-smith, with a quiet twinkle in his eye and the cheery tone of a good heart in his voice: "he jest about lives in that tree, an' there's generally suthin' there for him."

It was a spot to win a man's love, the spot the blacksmith had chosen for his temporary home, the little open had so sheltered and sheltering a look: to the south, east, north, mountain walls; to the west a vista, a suggestion of outlet, and a great friendliness of pine-trees. Two small brooks ran across the clearing. A thick line of bare, gray cotton-woods marked them now; in the summer they would be bowers of green, and the little bridges across them would be hid in thickets of foliage. The upper line of the southern mountain wall stood out against the sky in bold and fantastic shapes, endlessly sug-gestive. That rocks not hewn by men's hands should have such simil-itudes is marvellous. I have seen photographs of ruins in Edom and Palmyra which seem to be almost reproductions of these rocky summit outlines of some of our Colorado peaks.

A half-mile farther on we came upon the camp of the men who were building the road. "Camp" is an elastic word. In this case, it meant merely a small pine grove, two big fires, and some piles of blankets. Here the road ceased. As we halted, three dogs came bounding towards us, barking most furiously. One of them stopped suddenly, gave one searching look at me, put her tail between her legs, and with a pitiful yelp of terror turned and fled. I walked slowly after her; she would look back over her shoulder, turn, make one or two lunges at me, barking shrilly, then with the same yelp of terror run swiftly away; at last she grew brave enough to keep her face toward me, but continually backed away, alternating her bark of defiance with her yelp of terror in a way which was irresistibly ludicrous. We were utterly perplexed by her behavior until her master, as soon as he could speak for laughing, explained it.

"Yer see, that 'ere dog's never seen a woman afore. She was reared in the woods, an' I hain't never took her nowheres, an' thet's jest the fact on't; she dunno what to make of a woman."

It grew droller and droller. The other dogs were our good friends at once, leaped about us, snuffed us, and licked our hands as we spoke to them. Poor Bowser hung back and barked furiously with warning and menace whenever I patted one of the other dogs, but if I took a step nearer her she howled and fled in the most abject way.

Two men were baking bread, and there seemed a goodnatured rivalry between them.

"I've got a leetle too much soda in it," said one, as I peered curiously into his big bake-keetle, lifting the cover, "but his'n's all burnt on the top," with a contemptuous cock of his eye towards his fellow-baker. It is said to be very good, this impromptu bread, baked in a shapeless lump in an iron kettle, with coals underneath and coals on the lid above. It did not look so, however. I think I should choose the ovens of civilization.

The owner of my canine foe was a man some fifty-five or sixty years old. He had a striking face, a clear, blue-gray eye, with a rare mixture of decision and sentiment in it, a patriarchal gray beard, and a sensitive mouth. He wore a gray hat, broader-brimmed even than a Quaker's, and it added both picturesqueness and dignity to his appearance. His voice was so low, his intonation so good, that the uncultured speech seemed strangely out of place on his lips. He had lived in the woods "nigh eight year," sometimes in one part of the Territory, sometimes in another. He had been miner, hunter, farmer, and now road-builder. A very little talk with men of this sort usually draws from them some unexpected revelations of the motives or the incidents of their career. A long lonely life produces in the average mind a strange mixture of the taciturn and the confidential. The man of the wilderness will journey by your side whole days in silence; then, of a sudden, he will speak to you of matters which it would be, for you, utterly impossible to mention to a stranger. We soon learned the secret of this man's life in the woods. Nine years ago his wife had died. That broke up his farm home, and after that "all places seemed jest alike" to him, and "somehow" he "kinder took to the woods." What an unconscious tribute there is in that phrase to nature's power as a beneficent healer.

"There was another reason, too," he added. "My wife, she died o'consumption, hereditary, an' them two boys'd ha' gone the same way ef I hadn't kep' 'em out-o'-doors," pointing to two stalwart young men perhaps eighteen and twenty. "They hain't slep' under a roof for eight year, an' now they're as strong an' hearty as you'd wish to see." They were, indeed, and they may thank their father's wisdom for it.

Just beyond this camp was a cabin of fir boughs. Who that has not seen can conceive of the fragrant loveliness of a small house built entirely of fir boughs? It adds to the spice and the green and the airy lightness and the shelter of the pine-tree a something of the compactness and deftness and woven beauty of a bird's nest. I never weary of looking at it, outside and in: outside, each half-confined twig lifting its cross of soft, plumy ends and stirring a little in the wind, as it used to do when it grew on the tree; inside, the countless glints of blue sky showing through the boughs, as when one lies on his back under a low pine-tree and looks up. This cabin has only three sides built of boughs. The fourth is a high bowlder, which slants away at just the right angle to make a fire-place. The stone is of a soft, friable kind, and the fire has slowly eaten its way in, now and then cracking off a huge slice, until there is quite a fine "open Franklin" for the cabin. It draws well when the wind is in the right direction, as I can testify, for I have made fires in it. If the wind is from the east, it smokes, but I never heard of an open Franklin that did not.

The coming down over our new road is so unlike the going up that the very road seems changed. The beautiful triangular pictures of the distant plains are constantly before our eye, widening at each turn, and growing more and more distinct at each lower level we reach. The blue line of the divide in the northern horizon looks always like a solid line of blue. By what process a stretch of green timber land turns into a wall of lapis lazuli, does the science of optics teach?

It is nearly sunset as we descend. The plains look boundless. Their color is a soft mingling of pink and yellow and gray; each smallest hollow alike seem dimples on the smooth expanse. Here and there patches of ploughed land add their clear browns with a fine effect of dark mosaics on the light surface.

As we pass the bare slopes where the kinnikinnick is richest and greenest, we load our carriage with its lovely, shining mats. Below, on the soft pink plains, is a grave we love. It lies in the shade of great pines, on a low hill to the west of the town. Surely, never did a little colony find ready to its hand a lovelier burial-place than this.

Long ago there must have been watercourses among these low hills, else these pines could never have grown so high and strong. The watercourses are dried now, and only barren sands lie around the roots of the great trees, but still they live and flourish, as green in December as in June, and the wind in their branches chants endless chants above the graves.

This grave that we love lies, with four pines guarding it closely, on a westward slope which holds the very last rays of the setting sun. We look up from it to the glorious, snow-topped peaks which pierce the sky, and the way seems very short over which our friend has gone. The little mound is kept green with the faithful kin-nikinnick vines, and we bring them, now, from the highest slopes which our new road reaches, on the mountain our friend so loved.

Cheyenne Falls (now known as Seven Falls). From The
Crest of the Continent *(Chicago: R.R. Donnelly and
Sons, 1885).*

FOUR

Little Rose and the
House of the Snowy Range

*The mining town of Rosita had a special appeal for Jackson. Not only did
she write glowingly of it in "Little Rose and the House of the Snowy Range,"
but she also used it as a setting for a major section of NELLY'S SILVER
MINE. After Jackson's time, Rosita nearly disappeared. Located in Custer
County about fifteen miles east of Westcliff, Rosita was at its peak in the late
1870s when it was home to 2,000 residents. Much of the town burned down
in October 1881. Within ten years most of the residents had moved elsewhere, and Rosita was well on the way to becoming a ghost town. In more
recent years, however, the town has experienced a comeback. Fortunately,
Jackson captured the charm of the town during its heyday in her essay "Little
Rose and the House of the Snowy Range." This essay was first published in
the May 1878 issue of SCRIBNER'S MONTHLY MAGAZINE.*

Rosita, which being turned from Spanish into English means
Little Rose, is a mining camp in the silver region of the Sierra
Mojada, in southern Colorado. A legend runs that there was once
another "Little Rose," a beautiful woman of Mexico, who had a
Frenchman for a lover. When she died, her lover lost his wits and
journeyed aimlessly away to the north; he rambled on and on until
he came to this beautiful little nook, nestled among mountains, and
overlooking a great green valley a thousand feet below it. Here he
exclaimed, "Beautiful as Rosita!" and settled himself to live and die
on the spot.

A simpler and better authenticated explanation of the name
is, that when the miners first came, six years ago, into the gulches
where the town of Rosita now lies, they found several fine springs
of water, each spring in a thicket of wild roses. As they went to and
fro, from their huts to the springs, they found in the dainty blossoms a certain air of greeting, as of old inhabitants welcoming
new-comers. It seemed no more than courteous that the town

should be called after the name of the oldest and most aristocratic settler,—a kind of recognition which does not always result in so pleasing a name as Rosita (Thompkinsville, for instance, or Jenkins's Gulch). Little Rose, then, it became, and Little Rose it will remain. Not even a millionaire of mines will ever dare to dispute this vested title of the modest little flower. Each spring would brand him as a usurper, for the wild rose still queens it in the Sierra Mojada.

I suppose there may be many ways of approaching Rosita. I know only the one by which we went last June; going from Colorado Springs, first to Canyon City, by rail.

Canyon City lies at the mouth of the Grand Canyon by which the Arkansas River forces its way through the Wet Mountain range. It is a small town, which has always been hoping to be a large one. Since the Arkansas comes down this way from the great South Park, men thought they could carry and fetch goods on the same road; but the granite barrier is too much for them. Bold and rich must the railroad company be that will lay a track through this canyon. Canyon City has also many hot springs, highly medicinal; and it has hoped that the world would come to them to be cured of diseases. It has coal, too, in great quantity, and of good quality; and this seemed a certain element of prosperity. But, spite of all, Canyon City neither grows nor thrives, and wears always a certain indefinable look of depression and bad luck about it, just as men do when things go wrong with them year after year. It is surrounded on two sides by low foot-hills, which present bare fronts of the gloomiest shade of drab ever seen. One does not stop to ask if it be clay, sand, or rock, so overpowering is one's sense of the color. It would not seem that so neutral a tint could make a glare; but not even on the surfaces of white houses can the sun make so blinding and intolerable a glare as it does on the drab plains and drab foot-hills of Canyon City. One escapes from it with a sense of relief which seems at first disproportionate,—a quick exhilaration, such as is produced by passing suddenly from the society of a stupid person into that of a brilliant and witty one. You see at once how frightfully you were being bored. You had not realized it before. Through six miles of this drab glare we drove, in a south-westerly direction, then we set out for Rosita. On the outskirts of the town we passed the penitentiary,—also of a drab color,—a fine stone building. To liven things a little, the authorities have put the convicts into striped tights, black and white. The poor fellows were hewing, hammering, and wheeling drab stone, as we drove past. They looked droll enough,—like two-legged zebras prancing about.

The six miles of drab plain were relieved only by the cactus blossoms. These were abundant and beautiful, chiefly of the prickly pear variety, great mats of uncouth, bristling leaves, looking like oblong, green griddle-cakes, made thick and stuck full of pins, points out,—as repellant a plant as is to be found anywhere on the face of the earth; but lo! out of the edge of this thick and unseemly lobe springs a many-leaved chalice of satin sheen, graceful, nay, regal in its poise, in its quiet. No breeze stirs it; no sun wilts it; no other blossom rivals the lustrous transparency of its petals. Of all shades of yellow, from the palest cream-color up to the deepest tint of virgin gold; of all shades of pink, form a faint, hardly perceptible flush, up to a rose as clear and bright as that in the palm of a baby's hand. Myriads of these, full-blown, half-blown, and in bud, we saw on every rod of the six miles of desolate drab plains which we crossed below Canyon City. As soon as the road turned to the west and entered the foot-hills we began to climb; almost immediately we found ourselves on grand ledges. On these we wound and rose, and wound and rose, tier above tier, tier above tier, as one winds and climbs the tiers of the Coliseum in Rome; from each new ledge a grander off-look to the south and east; the whole wide plain wooded in spaces, with alternating intervals of smooth green fields; Pike's Peak and its range, majestic and snowy, in the northeastern horizon; countless peaks in the north; and, in the near foreground, Canyon City, redeemed from all its ugliness and bareness, nestled among its cotton-wood trees as a New England village nestles among its elms. It fills consciousness with delight almost too full, to look off at one minute upon grand mountain summits, and into distances so infinite one cannot even conjecture their limits,—see the peaks lost in clouds, and the plains melting into skies; and the next minute to look down on one's pathway and be dazzled by a succession of flowers almost as bewildering as the peaks and the plains. Here, on these rocky ledges, still grow the gold and pink cactus cups; and beside these, scarlet gilias, blue penstemons, white daisies and yellow spiraea, blue harebells and blue larkspur. This blue larkspur is the same which we see in old-fashioned gardens in New England. In Colorado it grows wild, side by side with the blue harebell, and behaves like it,—roots itself in crevices, and sways and waves in every wind.

The crowning beauty of the flower-show on these rocky ledges was a cactus, whose name I do not know. It is shaped and moulded like the sea-urchin, and grows sometimes as large as the wheel of a baby-carriage. Its lobes or sections are of clear apple-green, and thick set with long spines of glistening white. The flower is a many-leaved, tubular cup, of a deep, rich crimson color. They are thrown out at hap-hazard, apparently, anywhere on the lobes. You will often see ten, twelve, or even twenty of these blossoms on a single plant of only medium size, say, eight or ten inches in diameter. When we first saw one of these great, crimson-flowered cacti, wedged in like a cushion or flattened ball in the gnarled roots of an old cedar-bush, on the side of this rocky road, we halted in silent wonder, and looked first at it and then at each other. Afterward we grew wonted to their beauty; we even pulled several of them up bodily, and carried them home in a box; but this familiarity bred no contempt,—it only added to our admiration a terror which was uncomfortable. A live creature which could bite would be no harder to handle and carry. It has one single root growing out at its centre, like the root of a turnip; this root is long and slender; it must wriggle its way down among the rocks like a snake. By this root you can carry the cactus, and by this alone. Woe betide you if you can so much as attempt to tug, or lift, or carry it by its sides. You must pry it up with a stick or trowel till you can reach the root, grasp it by that handle, and carry it bottom side up, held off at a judicious distance from your legs.

At last we had climbed up to the last ledge, rounded the last point. Suddenly we saw before us, many hundred feet below us, a green well, into the mouth of which we looked down. There is nothing but a well to which I can compare the first view from these heights of the opening of Oak Creek Canyon. The sides of the well slant outward. Perhaps it is more like a huge funnel, little end down. The sun poured into these green depths, so full and warm that each needle on the fir-trees glittered, and a fine aromatic scent arose, as if spices were being brewed there. One small house stood in the clearing. It was only a rough-built thing, of unpainted pine; but Colorado pine is as yellow as gold, and if you do not know that it is pine, you might take it, at a little distance, for some rare and gleaming material which nobody but kings could afford to make houses of.

Down into this green well we dashed, on precipitous ledges as steep as that we had climbed. Once down at the bottom of the well, we stopped to look up and back. It seemed a marvel that there should be a way in or out. There are but two: the way we had come, scaling the ledges; and the way we were to go, keeping close to Oak Creek. Close indeed! The road clings to the creek as one blind might cling to a rope; for miles and miles they go hand in hand, cross and recross and change places, like partners in a dance, only to come again side by side. It would take botany and geology, and painting as well, to tell the truth of this exquisite Oak Creek Canyon. Its sides were a tangle of oak, beeches, willows, clematis, green-brier, and wild rose; underneath these, carpets of white violets and blue, yellow daisies and white, and great spaces of an orange-colored flower I never saw before, which looked like a lantana; a rich purple blossom also, for which I have neither name nor similitude. Above these banks and waving walls of flowers, were the immovable walls of rock, now in precipices, now in piles of bowlders, now in mountain-like masses. Often the canyon widens, and encloses, now a few acres of rich meadow-land, where a ranchman has built himself a little house, and begun a farm; now a desolate and arid tract, on which no human being will ever live. At all these openings there are glimpses of snowy peaks to the right and to the left. The road is literally in the mountains. At last,—and at last means nearly at sunset,—we reached the end of the canyon. It had widened and widened until, imperceptibly, it had ceased, and we were out in a vast open, with limitless distances stretching away in all directions. We were on a great plateau; we had climbed around, through, and come out on top of, the Sierra Mojada. We were on a plateau, yet the plateau was broken and uneven, heaved up into vast, billowy ovals and circles, which sometimes sharpened into ridges and were separated by ravines. It was a tenantless, soundless, well-nigh trackless wilderness. Our road had forsaken the creek, and there was no longer any guide to Rosita. Now and then we came to roads branching to right or left; no guide-posts told their destination, and in the silence and forsaken emptiness of these great spaces, all roads seemed alike inexplicable. In the west, a long, serrated line of snow-topped summits shone against the red sky. This was the grand Sangre di Cristo range, and by this we might partly know which way lay Rosita.

By a hesitating instinct, and not in any certainty, we groped along in that labyrinth of billowy hills and ravines, twilight settling fast upon the scene, and the vastness and the loneliness growing vaster and more lonely with each gathering shadow.

We were an hour too late. We had lingered too long among the flowers. Had we come out on this plateau in time to see the marshalling of the sunset, we should have looked down on Rosita all aglow with its reflection, and have seen the great Wet Mountain valley below like one long prism of emerald laid at the feet of the mountains which are called by the name of the "Blood of Christ."

It was dark when we saw the Rosita lights ahead, and there was a tone of unconfessed relief in the voice with which my companion said: "Ha! there is Rosita now!"

I think if I had driven down into a deep burrow of glow-worms in Brobdingnag, I should have had about the same sensations I had as we crept down into the black twinkling gulches of Rosita. When I saw them by daylight, I understood how they looked so weird by night, but at my first view of them they seemed uncanny indeed. The shifting forms of the miners seemed unhumanly grotesque, and their voices sounded strange and elfish.

"The House of the Snowy Range," they all replied, as we asked for the name of the best inn. "That's the one you'd like best. Strangers always go there."

"The House of the Snowy Range" was simple enough English, I perceived, the next morning, but that night it sounded to me mysterious and half terrifying, as if they had said, "Palace of the Ice King," or, "Home of the Spirits of the Frost."

Never was a house better named than the House of the Snowy Range. It is only an unpainted pine house, two stories high, built in the roughest way, and most scantily furnished. Considered only as a house, it is undeniable bare and forlorn; but it is never to be considered only as a house. It is the House of the Snowy Range. That means that as you sit on the roofless, unrailed, unplaned board piazza, you see in the west the great Sangre di Cristo range,— more peaks than you would think of counting, more peaks than you could count if you tried, for they are so dazzling white that they blind the eye which looks too long and steadily at them. These peaks range from ten thousand to fifteen thousand feet in height; they are all sharp-pointed and sharp-lined to the base: no curves, no confusion of over-lapping outlines. Of all the myriad peaks, lesser and greater, each one is distinct; the upper line made by the highest summits against the sky is sharply serrated, as if it were the teeth of a colossal saw; the whole front, as shown sloping to the east, is still a surface of sharp, distinct, pyramidal peaks, wedged in with each other in wonderful tiers and groupings. From the piazza of the House of the Snowy Range to the base of the nearest of these peaks is only five miles; but you look over at them through so marvellous a perspective that they seem sometimes nearer, sometimes much farther. They lie the other side of the great Wet Mountain valley. The House of the Snowy Range is one thousand feet above this valley, and gets its view of it between two near and rounding hills. From the piazza, therefore, you look at the Sangre di Cristo peaks across the mouth, as it were, of a huge, oval, emerald well, one thousand feet deep, yet illuminated with the clearest sunlight. It is an effect which can never be described. I am humiliated as I recall it and re-read these last few sentences. I think it would be the despair of the greatest painter that ever lived. What use, then, are words to convey it?

The Wet Mountain valley, or park, is thirty miles long and from four to five wide. It is one of the most fertile spots in Colorado. In July the meadow grasses grow higher than a man's knee, and the hill slopes are carpeted with flowers. It is full of little streams and never-failing springs, fed from the snows on the mountain wall to the west. Here are large farms, well tilled and fenced in, and with comfortable houses. The creeks are full of trout, and the mountain slopes are full of game. It ought to be a paradise coveted and sought for; but the sound of the pickaxe from the hills above them reaches the ears of the farmers, and makes them discontented with their slower gains. Man after man they are drawn away by the treacherous lure, and the broad, beautiful valley is still but thinly settled. This is a mistake; but it is a mistake that is destined to go on repeating itself forever in all mining countries. The contagion of the haste to be rich is as deadly as the contagion of a disease, and it is too impatient to take note of facts that might stay its fever. It is a simple matter of statistics, for instance, that in the regions of Georgetown and Central City the average miner is poor, while the man who sells him potatoes is well off. Yet for one man who sells him potatoes, twenty will go into a mine.

I am not sure, however, that it is wholly the lure of silver which draws men up form the green farms of Wet Mountain valley to the hills of Rosita. It might well be the spell of the little place itself. Fancy a half dozen high, conical hills, meeting at their bases, but sloping fast and far enough back to let their valleys be sunny and open; fancy these hills green to the very top, so that cattle go grazing higher and higher, till at the very summit they look no bigger than flies; fancy these hills shaded here and there with groves of pines and firs, so that one need never walk too far without shade; fancy between five and six hundred little houses, chiefly of the shining yellow pine, scattered irregularly over these hill-sides; remember that from the door-ways and windows of these houses a man may look off on the view I have described,— across a green valley one thousand feet below him, up to a range of snow-topped mountains fifteen thousand feet above him,—and does it not seem natural to love Rosita? Another most picturesque figure in the landscape is the contrast of color produced by the glittering piles of quartz thrown up at the mouths of the mines. There are over three hundred of these mines; they are dotted over the hill-sides, and each mine has its great pyramid of loose stone, which shines in the sun and is of a beautiful silvery gray color. The names of these mines are well-nigh incredible, and produce most bewildering effects when one hears them on every hand in familiar conversation. "Leviathan," "Lucille," "Columbus," "Hebe," "Elizabeth," "Essex," "Humboldt," "Buccaneer," "Montezuma," "Ferdinand," "Sunset," "Bald Hornet," "Silver Wing," "Evening Star," and "Hell and Six," are a few of them. Surely they indicate an amount and variety of taste and research very remarkable to be found in a small mining community.

On the morning after our arrival, we drove down into Wet Mountain valley, crossed it, and climbed high up on one of the lower peaks of the Sangre di Cristo range. From this point we looked back on the Sierra Mojada; it was a sea of green mountain-tops, not a bare or rocky summit among them. Rosita was out of sight, and, looking at its close-set hills, one who did not know would have said there was no room for a town there.

At our feet grew white strawberry-blossoms, the low Solomon's seal, and the dainty wild rose, as lovely, as perfect, and apparently as glad here, ten thousand feet above the sea, as they seem on a spring morning in New England's hills and woods.

Finding one's native flowers thousands of miles away from home seems to annihilate distance. To be transplanted seems the most natural thing in the world. Exile is not exile, if it be to a country where the wild rose can grow and a Snowy Range give benediction.

FIVE

A Colorado Woman's Museum

This essay grew out of a trip Jackson took to Boulder to see Martha Maxwell's Rocky Mountain Museum. Like Jackson, Maxwell was an educated and independent woman who felt drawn to Colorado. An avid naturalist and skilled taxidermist, Maxwell set out to create a museum that would exhibit specimens of some of the animals native to the Rocky Mountains. When building her displays, she attempted to re-create the animals' natural habitats. She also tried to place the animals in groupings that corresponded with the animal groupings that would be found in nature. At the time, this was a revolutionary approach to displaying animal specimens, and it helped attract attention to her museum when it opened in 1874. Jackson visited Maxwell's museum in 1875. This essay was first published in the October 1876 issue of ST. NICHOLAS.

You will ask yourselves, "What does that mean—a woman's museum?" and you will think, I suppose, that it means only a collection of curious things which some woman has bought and arranged in glass cases. Ah, it is quite different from that. I will try to tell you about it, and perhaps by the help of the pictures, and what I say, you will get some idea of how wonderful a museum it is.

There are many things in this museum—shells, minerals, coins, curious armor from Japan, queer garments from Alaska, tapa cloth from the Sandwich Islands, and a great many other curiosities, more than I can remember, or could have room in the ST. NICHOLAS to tell you about. I am going to tell you only about the stuffed animals and birds. These are the most interesting things in the museum, and the wonderful thing about them is, that they all were stuffed and many of them killed by the woman who owns the museum. Think of that!—of a woman's being able to fire her rifle as well as any old hunter could, and then, after she has brought down her bear or her wild-cat, knowing how to skin it and stuff it so that it looks exactly as if it were alive. This is really the most wonderful thing of all. You know very well how stuffed animals generally look. You know they are dead as far off as you can see them; but these animals all look as if they might walk off any minute they liked. Mrs. Maxwell (that is the name of the woman who has made this remarkable museum) is really a sculptor of animals. Most people who stuff animals, take the skin, I fancy, very much as a sausage-maker takes a sausage-skin, and simply cram into it as much as it will hold without bursting, for it is very elastic. I have heard that the skin of any animal will bear stretching till it is one-third larger than the animal was when alive. Well, if a dead animal's skin is as elastic as that, it is very easy to see how, in stuffing it, one might entirely spoil its shape and make it look unnatural. I have seen many a stuffed animal that didn't look any more like what it was when it was alive, than a sausage looks like a pig!

Mrs. Maxwell stuffs her animals on a totally different plan, and this is why I say she is a sculptor of animals. The first thing she does is to mold the animal out of plaster, of the size and in the position she wishes. Then she fits the skin on the plaster shape. In the case of large animals, such as the bison or buffalo, she makes the figure partly of hay as well as of plaster, and what sort of a bison this

THE BISON.

results in you can see by the picture. I have never seen a live bison, but if I ever do, I do not believe he will put his head down and glare out from under his horns in one whit fiercer a way than this one does.

When I went into Mrs. Maxwell's museum, the first thing that caught my eye was a little black and tan terrier dog, lying under the table. He was a remarkably pretty dog, and, as we walked toward him, he fixed his eyes on us with a very keen and suspicious look, I thought. But he did not stir. I said to myself, "Why, what is the matter with that dog? Why doesn't he get up?" And then I saw that he was only a stuffed dog! Then I wished I had had a real live dog with me, to see if he wouldn't have been deceived too. I think he would.

Now I must tell you how the large groups of animals are arranged, for one reason that they look so natural is that Mrs. Maxwell has made an "outdoors" for them at one end of the room. She has had built up a sort of wooden frame-work, in the shape of rocks. This is covered with a coarse canvas cloth, which has been prepared with glue or some sticky substance. Over this, coarse shining sand of a dark gray color is sprinkled thick; and as the cloth is sticky, the sand remains. At a very little distance nobody would know the rocks from real rocks of dark gray stone. Then she has set real pine and fir trees among them, and little clumps of grasses, and mounds of real dirt. You can see all these in the pictures.

One of the most effective groups is the one where you see a large animal springing from a tree. That is a mountain lion. They are often found in the woods of Colorado. He is leaping down in the pursuit of the poor stag, which you see just to the right. The stag has run till he can run no longer; he is falling down on his knees, and his tongue is lolling out of his mouth, he is so out of breath. Just below these is a happy family of deer—father and mother and two little fawns. The little fawns are only a few days old. They are beautifully mottled with white spots on light brown.

A GROUP OF ANIMALS.

The doe is bending her neck down and licking one of them as affectionately as a cat licks her kitten, and father, just behind, is holding up his head and looking off very proudly, as much as to say, "Who's got a prettier family than I have, I'd like to know!"

Below them are some porcupines, muskrats, weasels, and small creatures; and off on the left, two splendid great bears, one a grizzly fellow that you wouldn't like to meet in the woods. Once, when I was riding in the woods on the rim of the Yosemite Valley, I saw the tracks of a grizzly bear in the sand. He had been there only a short time before us, for the tracks were very fresh. They looked just like the print of a giant's mittens, and they made us all feel very uncomfortable.

Another happy family in this museum is that of the mountain sheep—father, mother, and an only child. The father looks like a huge goat, with queer curling horns. The Colorado hunters see a great many like him, scrambling around on the rocks in high and precipitous places. Below him in the group is a fox, just ready to spring on a mouse, and near by is a wild-cat creeping out of a cave, and making up her mind to have a gray rabbit in front of her for dinner.

This group is not shown you, but you will have many a good laugh over those that the engraver has copied so admirably. As I sit

"THE MOONLIGHT WALK."

here in my Colorado home, it does my very heart good to think how many thousand children will shout over the pictures of the monkeys playing cards, and of the little house out of which Mr. Brown Squirrel and Miss Yellow Duckling are coming arm-in-arm to take a walk. Mrs. Maxwell calls this "The Moonlight Walk." The duckling is all covered with bright yellow down, and is not more than three or four inches high.

I think she must have been caught as soon as she was fairly out of the shell. The squirrel is a head taller, as he ought to be, and has the most comical air of gallant protection toward his lady-love. They both look so droll, that nobody can help laughing at the first sight of them.

The monkeys, too, are very droll. One old fellow, with a pipe in his mouth, is scratching his head in his perplexity to know what card to play. The one next him is peering out from behind his cards, and watching the opposite monkey's face most keenly, to discover, if he can, what cards he holds; and while they are all too absorbed in their game to see what is going on, a sly little rascal of a monkey is climbing up the leg of the table and taking their goblet.

AN EXCITING GAME.

But of all the groups, I am not sure that the prairie-dog's hole is not the very best. I see dozens of such mounds every day when I drive out, in Colorado, and on all the warm sunshiny days I see just such little prairie-dogs popping their heads out of the hole to find out who is going by, and there are always one or two more courageous ones who sit up on their haunches and look boldly at us. I have never happened to see either an owl or a rattlesnake on the mounds, but it is a well-known fact that they live in them. Mrs. Maxwell says she has often seen them come out of the holes, but "what their arrangements are for living there" she does not know, and nobody ever can know.

There would not be room here to tell you about half of the

THE PRAIRIE-DOG'S MOUND.

animals, neither can I tell you about the stuffed birds. They are as wonderful as the animals, and there are hundreds of them—all the birds of Colorado, and a great many of other countries. You will see by the two groups on the next page, however, that they look just as natural as the animals, and not at all like the usual double guidepost arrangements of stuffed birds. They look like flocks that had just alighted on a dead tree. You must not forget to look at the old mother-quail at the foot of one of these trees, with her little chickens all about her, one on her back and one sticking its head out through her wing. You'd think, if you called, "Chick, chick, chick," they'd all come running to get corn.

GROUP OF BIRDS, NO. I.

Now I can tell you about only two more things—an owl and a bird's nest. The owl is alive; it is Mrs. Maxwell's pet. She had two, but, unfortunately, her live bear ate up one of them. She found these young owls in their nest, when they were tiny little creatures, all covered with soft fluffy down. I saw them just after she found them, a year ago. They looked like little balls of gray feathers, with two big glass beads sewed on them for eyes. Now, this little owl's downy feathers are all smooth and flat, and two small feather horns, looking just like cats' ears, have grown out of his head; and though he is only a few inches high, he looks as wise as any owl in the world. If you rub him gently on his head between his ears, he shuts his eyes right up and goes to sleep; but however sound asleep he seems to be, if you touch him on his back ever so lightly, he wakes up, makes a sharp angry noise, and whirls round and round quick as lightning, to bite your finger. Whenever he did this, he reminded me of a kitten going round and round after its tail. His head seems to be set on a pivot, for, without moving his body, he can turn it clear round, and see anything he wants to see behind him. He can also wink with one eye, while the other eye looks at you in a fixed stare. When he does this, his expression is more impudent than any human face could possibly wear. We laughed till the tears came into our eyes, watching this comical little creature.

I think that tears almost came into my eyes also when I looked at the bird's nest I am going to tell you of. They would not have been tears from laughter, however; they would have been tears of tender wonder and admiration for the little bird who built it.

Up in the mountains some thirty miles northwest of Denver is a wild canyon called Boulder Canyon. A canyon is a steep-sided valley between two mountains; sometimes it is little more than a rift between two precipices of rock. In this Boulder Canyon there is just room for a carriage-road and a swift little river, which is hardly more than a brook. Half-way down this canyon another canyon opens into it, and another swift little brook comes leaping down and fairly bounds into the first one. A few rods up this second canyon is a fine fall, or succession of falls, known as Boulder Falls. One day, a young man, sitting near these falls, saw a small bird fly apparently in the falling sheet of water. Presently it came back, was gone a short time, returned, bringing something in its beak, and second time darted into the spray and disappeared. This young

GROUP OF BIRDS, NO. 2.

man was an enthusiastic lover of natural history, and he determined to find out what that bird was doing behind Boulder Falls. If you only could see the place, you would wonder he ever had courage to venture where he did. He had to build a sort of bridge, and he had to wade in between rocks, where the stream was swift enough to knock him senseless in a very few minutes if he lost his footing; he really risked his life to track that little bird to her home. And do you not think he was rewarded when he found, snugly stowed away in a hollow behind the sheet of falling water, the nest, with the young birds in it?

Poor little bird! One would have thought she had found the very safest sort of a place which the whole world could offer; and so she had—safe against storm, against wild animals, against sportsmen, against everything except a naturalist!

The nest is made of clay and green moss; its mouth looks like the mouth of an old-fashioned brick oven; and there are all the little birds, with their mouths wide open, just as they waited for their mother to bring them food that day. The mother, too, he shot and brought away with the beautiful little house she had built. I think I could not have had the heart to kill her, even for the sake of the science of natural history. However, many things which seem cruel in themselves, must be done, or else we should never learn the truth about the wonderful creatures of which the world is full. But while I stood looking at the nest, I would have given a great deal to put it back under Boulder Falls again, with some happy little live birds in it, getting their dinner from their wet and dripping mamma. And the more I thought about it, the more I wondered whether it were really right for us ever to kill a living creature except for food. If there were a race of beings as much larger and stronger than we are, as we are than the birds, we would think it pretty hard, would we not, if they were in the habit of pulling our houses down over our heads, and killing us and our children, merely that they might classify us and label us and keep us in their museums?

Ranch Life in Colorado

Jackson visited many ranches while living in Colorado. In this article she described three types of ranches: cattle ranches, sheep ranches, and farm ranches. "Ranch Life in Colorado" first appeared in the May 20, 1880, issue of THE YOUTH'S COMPANION.

The word "ranch" is a contraction of the Spanish word "rancho," which means "a hut covered with branches or thatch for herds-men," or "a farming establishment for the raising of horses and cattle."

In Colorado, and in California as well, the word has come to be applied indiscriminately to all farms, whether the land be used for grazing or for agricultural purposes.

The word has a seductive sound. It suggests beautiful and picturesque surroundings, green trees, running streams, and a life of freedom and plenty; and I shall not soon forget the disappointment with which I first looked on a Colorado ranch.

A small, unpainted house, a story and a half high; a few out-buildings built of logs in the roughest manner; no fences; not a tree in sight; not a bush; chips and other litter all around; tin cans lying about in abundance; a most desolate-looking spot, with discomfort and deprivation staring you in the face at every point.

This was a cattle ranch. The proprietor of it owned several thousand head of cattle.

He himself lived in a good house in Colorado Springs. This is the most comfortable way to keep a ranch; put a man, or men, in charge of it, and live yourself wherever you please, visiting the ranch often enough to see that things are in order. But, of course, this method is possible only to persons with means.

There are three sorts of ranches in Colorado: sheep ranches, cattle ranches, and farm ranches.

Cattle Ranches

The cattle interest is far the largest of the three. It is estimated that eight millions of money are invested in this business.

The principal grazing sections in the State are along the Platte, the Arkansas, and the Republican Rivers, but the plains in all sections are thus utilized.

Some of the Parks lying high up among the mountains also afford fine ranges. To the eye of a stranger, nothing could look more unsuited for grazing than the bare brown stretches of the Colorado plains.

But there is a sweetness and a nutrition in the low dried grasses which is wonderful. No hay that is made can compare with these grasses dried where they stand, and ready to be nibbled all winter.

Again, to a stranger, nothing could seem more improbable than that cattle should thrive, running all winter long unsheltered, uncared for, in a country where the mercury frequently falls at night to zero, and below, and where snow frequently covers the ground to several inches depth. But the facts show that cattle do thrive under these conditions.

They are very thin in the spring, and an exceptionally severe snow-storm in March or April will kill off some of the feeblest ones; but at the end of the year they make, on the whole, fair returns, and there are many cattle-men in the State who are growing steadily rich.

Sheep Ranches

The same is true of the sheep-men, though this business is subject to greater risks and fluctuations. When heavy snow-storms come, sheep are helpless; they are silly also, and sometimes in a single flock, hundreds will be stifled to death by their trampling each other under foot, in haste to get food which has been thrown down for them when they have been driven in after a long storm.

This last winter has been, in some parts of Colorado, exceptionally severe, and thousands of sheep have perished in the snow.

The sheep-men have taken warning, and are putting up sheds on a large scale.

It would seem a simple matter of humanity, as well as policy, to provide them. Cattle can run before a storm, and will often, it is said, run forty miles to escape one; but the poor little sheep are too clumsy and slow; they are soon snowed in and under.

It is estimated that there are between five and six millions of dollars invested in the sheep business in the State, and Colorado wool is steadily growing in favor with manufacturers.

Farm Ranches

The agricultural interest in Colorado can never be a large one. It is a marvel that farmers will pass by the rich lands of Kansas to settle in a country where cold nights kill corn, and land must be irrigated to produce anything.

Wheat is the only grain crop on which it is worth while to count. Wheat does well. So do barley and oats; grass in valleys is abundant and good; and potatoes grow to a large size, and are excellent.

But the farmer has to work too hard. The trouble of making irrigating ditches and keeping up the supply of water is a serious addition to his labors. He will make at the best but a living, and that not a generous one.

To be content with this in a country where he sees men on all sides growing steadily rich by cattle or sheep, or making big fortunes in mines, a man must be either very lazy or very philosophical. In the ultimate future of Colorado, her industries and those of her neighboring States will, no doubt, be adjusted relatively to each other. She will make silver and gold, and they will send food to her.

Life on the larger and more remote ranches is lonely and monotonous to a degree which, it must be admitted, can hardly be wholesome for either mind or body.

The daily life of a herder of sheep, for instance, seems but one shade above that of the sheep themselves. He takes his flock out at daybreak, stands or lies still, watching them while they feed;

drives them back to the ranch at night; cooks his own supper, washes the dishes, and goes to bed at nine o'clock, too tired to keep awake longer. This routine is varied by an interval of very hard work in the shearing season, and during the weeks when the lambs are born in the spring.

If ranch is near a town of size, he goes, perhaps once a week, to that town to buy what he needs; but the larger ranches are all remote from towns, and must necessarily be so, to secure sufficient range for large flocks and herds.

For a ranch sixty, seventy, or a hundred miles distant from its centre of supplies, purchases must be made by wholesale two or three times a year, and the ranchmen will have no intercourse with the world, except at these times, and when chance travellers pass by their place. A primitive and genuine hospitality is kept on most ranches; all travellers feel free to stop at them; and by no means the least of the fatigues of the ranchman's life is the preparing meals at any time for as many as happen to come.

These are some of the drawbacks on ranch life.

On the other hand, there are advantages by no means to be scorned; open air, year in and year out; freedom from all conventional and troublesome customs; independence, and the indefinable exhilaration, which almost all men find in a wild and untrammelled life.

The cattle-men for a great part of the year have little to do, except to keep their buildings in order, and attend to the few animals they keep with them. When the cattle are to be gathered together, branded and counted, or driven from one range to another, then the cattle-man rides, day after day, as madly as a Bedouin in the desert.

There is probably no better riding than can be seen at the summer "Round ups," as they are called, where dozens of vast herds of cattle have been gradually driven in from their ranges and collected in a dense mass in some open place, for the owners to pick out their respective cattle.

Any cow or steer found unbranded then can be taken possession of by anyone; such cattle are called Mavericks (for what rea-

son, I cannot learn), and there are more of them than would be supposed; they might be called Ishmaelites among cattle.

As the ranchman prospers he adds building after building to
his ranch. You may read the history of many ranches in the successive
stages of building, from the roughest of log cabins, which was at first
the dwelling, and is now merely and outhouse for tools, implements,
etc., up to the two-story wooden house, possibly clapboarded, which
the ranchman's wife takes pride, and in which you will find one or more
carpeted rooms, a rocking-chair or two, and a newspaper or magazine.

I know one ranch, a sheep ranch, in which the record runs
farther back than the log home; it runs back to a "dug out," a sort of
compromise between a cave and a huge oblong ant-hill, in which the
resolute sheep-man lived, or rather burrowed, for more than a year,
when he began his Colorado life like David, with a "few sheep in the
wilderness." Now he is the owner of two ranches, and many thousand sheep; but he has paid, by a permanently impaired digestion,
the penalty for the months he spent in the "dug out," eating scanty
and poor food.

The one chief and greatest objection to ranch life, as it is in
Colorado at present, is the unwholesome food.

This need not be so bad, but there seems to be an unconquerable tendency in men living lonely and isolated lives, and doing
with their own hands all the work to be done in the house, to shirk
cooking, adopt the easiest methods, and fall into a dreary monotony
of diet which is unwholesome.

The difficulty of procuring any variety of fresh meats, also,
is another trouble which it is easier to evade by a perpetual recourse
to ham and bacon than in any other way.

The trouble of milking cows and making butter is also very
easily evaded by going without both butter and milk; and it is no
uncommon thing to find a ranchman owning many hundreds of cows
and not milking one. All of these things are to be taken account by
invalids, who are often recommended, in a haphazard way, to "go out
on some ranch and rough it for a year."

It would be a very exceptional invalid, or a very exceptional ranch, where there would not be more lost, by reason of bad food, than would be gained by the out-door life.

But after all is said and summed, for and against ranch life, there remains a certain element in it which can be neither said nor summed; and whose worth each individual will reckon at his own valuation, and cannot safely estimate for any other man. It is the nearness to nature, and the remoteness from man; all of which goes to make up his out-door life.

What the Bedouin knows of the desert, he could never tell; and the Colorado ranchman would probably find it quite as hard to give reasons for his love of ranch life.

SEVEN

Health Resorts in Colorado

In the first half of this essay, Jackson described three of the state's most popular health resorts: Manitou Springs, Cañon City, and Idaho Springs. She concluded this piece, however, with an interesting comparison of Colorado Springs and Denver. Although she attempted to be even-handed in her accounts of thise two communities, she did not succeed in hiding her preference for Colorado Springs. "Health Resorts in Colorado" was published in the May 13, 1880, issue of THE YOUTH'S COMPANION.

The places in Colorado which come most properly under this head are Manitou, Cañon City, and Idaho Springs.

Manitou is by far the pleasantest of the three places I have named. It is a little hamlet nestled among the foothills at the base of Pike's Peak.

It is in the mouth of Ute Pass, which is one of the most beautiful short passes in the Rocky Mountains.

To reach Manitou, you go by the Denver and Rio Grande Railroad from Denver to Colorado Springs. Stages run from Colorado Springs to Manitou on the arrival of every train, and the distances is only about five miles.

There are two beautiful Cañons within easy walking distance from Manitou; through one of these a trail has been made leading up to the top of Pike's Peak.

The famous "Garden of the Gods," also, lies only about two miles away. The Fountain Creek, a pretty and swift little stream, runs through the centre of the village.

There are three large hotels and several boarding houses here, all of which in summer are crowed to overflowing with visitors. The advantages of Manitou for invalids are, that it is sheltered from winds, that it has pleasant and shady walks along the brook, that the hotels are better than the average hotels in Colorado, and that there are several sorts of medicinal water close at hand.

The disadvantages are that, owing to the high hills around it, the place gets in the winter an hour and a half less sunshine per day than the town of Colorado Springs, only five miles distant, that it is for the same reason sometimes hot and close in the summer, and is very dusty. There is now and then an invalid who finds the dampness from the brook objectionable; and all invalids find the throng of summer visitors wearisome and oppressive.

In July and August, Manitou is like Newport or Saratoga, except that there is not so much fashion. A band plays every evening at the hotels, and that amusement known among Americans as "A Hop" occurs every week. Of course, under such circumstances no one can have the quite, the attention, or the food which an invalid needs.

Cañon City is not a city at all, but a small village lying at the mouth of the Grand Cañon of the Arkansas, about fifty miles southwest of Colorado Springs.

To reach it, you go by the Denver and Rio Grande Railroad from Denver to Pueblo; or can come from the East direct to Pueblo by the Atchison, Topeka and Santa Fe Railroad. At Pueblo, a branch of the Denver and Rio Grande Railroad runs to Cañon City.

The land is built on the banks of the Arkansas River, which comes out here from the "Grand Cañon," by which it has cut its way through the mountains.

This Cañon is one of the grandest sights in Colorado, and excursions to it are among the pleasantest features of life in Cañon City.

The town is dull and uninteresting; and the sandy cliffs, or buttes, to the back of it, are of a light drab color, which makes, under the hot Colorado sun, a glare almost as intolerable as that of white marble.

There is one very fair hotel there, and board can be had in a few of the private families.

The advantages of Cañon City for invalids are, that it is far enough to the South to be decidedly warmer in winter than either Manitou or Idaho; it is entirely sheltered from the north and northwest winds; the altitude is less, and the air is made moister by the nearness of the river, and therefore, for some invalids, much wholesomer, being less electric and exciting. There are pleasant drives and excursions into the near mountain; and for botanists, the flora of the region is of itself an occupation.

The disadvantages are that it is very hot in summer, and very dull at times; and the immediate views are not beautiful and interesting, like those at Manitou. The river water, also, which is the water drunk in the town, is often muddy and disagreeable.

Idaho is a little village in the mountains, a half day's journey by rail and stage northwest from Denver.

To reach it, you go by the Colorado Central Railroad, three or four hours from Denver, through the celebrated Clear Creek Cañon, which contains some of the grandest scenery in the State. The village is surrounded by hills, and there is a little brook running through it, as at Manitou, but owing to the greater altitude and poorer soil, there is much less foliage; and the place never looks so green and attractive as Manitou.

There is one good hotel and, connected with it, several cottages which are occupied by visitors. In summer the place is crowded with people, largely people from Denver seeking a refuge from the intolerable heat of that sun-smitten city.

There are very complete arrangements for baths at Idaho, much more so than at Cañon City or Manitou. The temperature of the water ranges from 70° to 110° Fahrenheit, and it is very largely impregnated with soda.

The advantages of Idaho are its sheltered situation, making it much warmer in the winter than most places which are so high; the vicinity of grand scenery and mining regions of great interest; and a hotel much better than the average Colorado hotel.

The disadvantages are the altitude (eight thousand feet),

which is too great for many patients, the extreme quiet and dulness of the place in winter, and its dust in summer.

There are several other points in Colorado at which mineral springs are found, and to which invalids have found their way; Morrison Springs, at Morrison, twelve miles west of Denver, on the Denver and South Park Railroad; the Hot Sulphur Springs in Middle Park and in South Park; the Cottonwood Hot Springs, on the Cottonwood branch of the Arkansas River, ninety miles west of the town of Colorado Springs, and the Poncho Hot Springs, situated in the Poncho Pass, in Lake County,—all these are sulphur springs, some hot and some cold; in none of these places, however, have arrangements yet been made at all complete or comfortable for the accommodation of invalids.

Of the other places in Colorado suitable for invalids seeking simply the climate influences, and not wishing to drink or bathe in medicinal waters, the city of Denver and the town of Colorado Springs are the chief. The merits of these two places are so warmly upheld by their respective advocates that it is almost dangerous to discuss them in either place, and perhaps well-nigh impossible for a person who likes one to do justice to the other. Certainly no one ever liked both.

Denver is a city with some twenty thousand inhabitants. Colorado Springs is a village (called a city), with not more than four thousand. Denver has big hotels, big shops, sidewalks (chiefly wooden), a theatre, concert-halls, billiard-rooms. Colorado Springs has two or three small hotels (as poor as Denver's big ones), a few small shops, grass-bordered paths, one town-hall, one billiard-room, and no whiskey-saloon.

Denver is rich; there are plenty of people there who have made big fortunes, built big house, and keep fast horses. A certain unenlightened extravagance is very noticeable. Showy clothes and ostentatious entertainment are common.

The expression of the city and its people would strike any Eastern traveller, walking up and down its streets for a few days, as being crude, fast, and flashy, redeemed to a degree by evident activity, energy, success, and a disposition to do everything in a liberal, and so far as things are understood, elegant manner. It has, in short, all the faults, foibles, and excellencies of a new rich Western city.

Colorado Springs is not rich. There is not in the town a man who would be called rich in New York. There are no big houses; there is no fast living; its ways are country ways; showy clothes and ostentatious entertainment would be ridiculous.

The whole expression of the town strikes travellers from the Eastern States as being like that of a New England village; small, neatly kept, comfortable homes; and the two biggest buildings in town are a Deaf and Dumb Asylum and a stone schoolhouse; a handsome college building, which is fast going up, also of stone, will, when it is completed, add still more to the New England look of the town.

In the matter of climate there is, perhaps, not so much difference between the two places as their respective advocates claim, but to hear the assertions on both sides, one would think that either one or the other place must prove fatal to most invalids.

Denver is a few hundred feet lower than the Springs; this is for many invalids a gain. Denver is colder in winter, and hotter in summer; it lies open and unsheltered on the plains; the mountains thirty miles away. Colorado Springs lies close to the base of the Pike's Peak range, sheltered by the Divide, a table-land eight thousand feet high, from winds from the north.

In the matter of scenery, immediately surrounding, or easily accessible, it would seem that there could be no claim set up for Denver, in comparison with Colorado Springs.

Yet there are those who assert that the one grand view of the main range, which is, no doubt, simply superb from Denver, more than outweighs all the picturesque beauty of the surroundings of the Springs. But to a true lover of nature, no one single view, however grand and however varied by changing atmospheric effects, can be so sufficing and so inexhaustible in pleasure as a region full of beautiful views, streams, woods, ravines, and climbable mountains, such as are to be enjoyed in the near neighborhood of Colorado Springs.

There are ten beautiful Cañons within an easy day's excursion from the town; most of them within reach by an afternoon's drive. There is the famous "Garden of the Gods," and "Monument Park;" there is Cheyenne Mountain, with its numerous promontory-like spurs, covered with grand pines, into the shade of which one can drive in an hour and a half from the town.

The relief, the blessing of this, after a scorching day of Colorado sunshine, cannot be told, neither is it possible to put in words the perpetual blessing to a lover of mountains of their near presence, friendliness, and shelter.

The elements of choice for invalids between Denver and Colorado Springs as a place of sojourn are easily summed up

The person who is accustomed to city routines, to depending upon people who like noise and movement, and has not learned to find occupation and delight in out-door life, would far better stay in Denver. He will be bored at Colorado Springs, and not know what to do with himself there.

The person who likes quiet, has resources within himself, is content with only a moderate and informal social life, and loves to drive, ride, and ramble in wild places, who can spend whole days happily with a friend, a book, a pine-tree, and the sky over his head, would better come straight to Colorado Springs. He will be bored and irritated in Denver, and not know what to do with himself there.

EIGHT

Health-Seeking in Colorado

In "Health-Seeking in Colorado," Jackson tried to explain why so many people moved to Colorado to improve their health. Since she knew many such people, she was able to make some keen observations about the experiences that these people had when they relocated to Colorado. She focused on how Colorado's climate affected the health of these people, but she also commented on how transplanted Easterners coped with Colorado's frontier lifestyle. This piece ran in the May 6, 1880, issue of THE YOUTH'S COMPANION.

A ll that a man hath will he give for his life," is as true now as it was in the days of Job, and one of the saddest spectacles which the earth affords today is the melancholy caravan of invalids journeying hither or thither in search of a man, or an air, that can prolong their days a little.

Within the last few years Colorado has come much into notice as a place of resort for invalids, chiefly for invalids suffering from asthma or consumption. Rash and unfounded generalizations have been widely scattered by newspaper correspondents; the numbers of cures have been exaggerated; the advantages of the climate have been over-stated. Its disadvantages have not been mentioned. For these reasons there is today a steady influx into the State of men and women who are leaving comfortable homes in the East, sacrificing assured incomes from professions or trades, and exposing themselves to all sorts of hardships and deprivations under the belief or hope that "Colorado will cure" them.

It is plain that there must be a genuine and substantial cause for such a movement as this; but it would save disappointment to vast numbers of people if it were generally and accurately known just what is, and what is not, to be expected from the Colorado climate; just what can be, and what cannot be done in Colorado; and so far as is possible by general statements, what course an invalid coming here had better pursue.

The Climate of Colorado

For the benefit, then, of persons who from sickness are under the necessity of seeking a change of climate, let me try to answer the question, what is, and what is not, to be expected from the Colorado climate.

It is not specifically curative. It is not a medicine. It can often arrest consumption, in the earlier stages of that disease, simply because the air is so dry that the lung tissues cannot go on altering. Ulcers on internal surfaces dry up, just as the external skin dries up when deprived of moisture.

Owing to this, the disease is arrested; nature has a chance to attend to her own instinctive healing; the patient is better; gains strength; feels himself saved.

Often after this result is secured the patient goes back East. Of course, he breaks down again in a few months with the same or with worse trouble, and then it is said that Colorado did not do him any real good after all.

The trouble was not with Colorado, but the man and his friends had expected too much. He might have lived to a good old age in Colorado. While he was there his disease was like an enemy whose weapons were taken away, and whose hands were tied. Going back to the lower attitude and moister air, he freed his enemy and put the weapons into his hands again.

Asthma and Consumption

In the case of asthma, which is the only disease of which it is safe to say that it is nearly always relieved in Colorado, what I have said about a change of climate is also true.

The asthmatic patient breathes here with ease. He says, "I am well." So long as he stays in Colorado, Colorado will compel his lungs to do him good service, but she gives no guaranteed passports to asthmatics to go beyond her lines.

In the cases of more advanced consumption, there is, of course, less benefit to be expected from the climate of Colorado. Still there are many persons living here in fairly comfortable health, able to do some work, who have very serious organic disease. They will probably die of consumption in Colorado, but it will be several years later than they would have died in the East.

Debility

Perhaps the invalids, next to the asthmatics, who are surest to be helped here in Colorado are those suffering from general debility and prostration.

There is a marvellous tonic in the dry air and in the sunshine. But to reap this benefit the weakened patients must lead outdoor lives, and obey strictly all the laws of health, which in nine cases out of ten they have been in the habit of breaking at home.

And this brings me to the head of what can and cannot be done in Colorado.

Inconveniencies

What inconveniences and drawbacks must a patient encounter in Colorado? An invalid cannot get the food he ought to have, unless he keeps house. The hotels and boarding-houses are, as a rule, poor.

This is not for lack of good food in the markets; it is owing to the fact that the standard of cooking in Colorado is low.

Opportunities of Employment

If the invalid needs to support himself, he will find it a hard thing to do. The country is new. The higher needs of society are yet not much recognized, and the lower are amply met.

A delicate and fastidious man or woman—and consumptives are almost always both—needing to earn money in Colorado, is at a sore disadvantage. For one situation for a teacher or minister, for one chance of earning money by painting, giving lessons, sewing, singing, or writing, there are scores of persons who are seeking such employments.

A man who can dig in a mine, work in a carpenter's shop; a woman who can (or will) take a situation as house servant here,—can command work and earn very high wages. Few others can. I get letters every month asking if there is any way for an invalid to earn a living here, —to earn even his board; and I have but one reply to make, that Colorado is a very hard country in every way for a person without means.

A few of the bare necessaries of life—beef, flour, coal—are cheap. Everything that can be called a luxury is dear. Muscle is in demand; money is in demand; brain-work and accomplishments are not.

If the invalid needs amusements, if he is a person without internal resources, accustomed to depend on the excitements and pleasures of city life, he will be badly off in Colorado. Nothing but a strong love of nature, and a firmly fixed habit of being happy in a quiet life, can make a person contented in Colorado.

What Can a Patient Do?

Now let me tell you what the invalid can do. He can spend more days in the open air in the course of a calendar year than he can in any climate in the world, unless it be that of Madeira. He can ride; he can drive; he can live in a tent; he can botanize in one of the most interesting floras in the world; he can geologize in a field full of perplexing interest; he can study human nature in new and varied aspects. If he is strong enough, and has the pecuniary means, he can visit the mining towns, and can see there phases of life which he can see nowhere except in mining districts. He can climb mountains fourteen thousand feet high; he can explore canyons twelve hundred deep.

If he has capital at command, he can invest some of it in sheep or cattle; and either put them under the care of a competent man, or take charge of them himself.

He can live in a small shanty, and do his own cooking; and if he has sufficient pluck and sense of humor to enjoy the situation, he will gain more, perhaps, in that way of life than in any other.

He can buy a camping outfit, and travel for four or five months in the year, sleeping in a tent every night. If he likes this, it will do him good. If he hates it, it will do him harm.

Who Should not go to Colorado

There is one thing that is not generally known, but which ought to be by all persons who think of coming to Colorado. It is the effect of the rarefied air upon the action of the heart. The pulse-beat is from ten to twelve per minute quicker here than at the sea-level.

This stimulus to circulation, while it is in many cases one of the beneficial agencies in the Colorado air, is in other cases very injurious. Persons with any form of heart-disease, or with any tendency to it, should never come here.

The electric conditions are also very peculiar, and as yet little understood. Some nervous persons are unable to sleep, and are obliged to go away in consequence.

The severe wind-storms which prevail in March and April, and occur occasionally in all other parts of the year, have a very seriously disturbing influence upon many people, causing in some great sleeplessness and a vague but intolerable discomfort; causing in others unconquerable drowsiness, so that they are obliged to go to sleep even in the middle of the day, as soon as the winds begin to blow. It is, of course, impossible in so short an article as this to give any minute details of Colorado life, or to give more than the briefest suggestions as to the effects of the climate. But I think I have said enough to partially give the information needed by many who are thinking of seeking a temporary home here.

I cannot better sum up the results of my own five years' observation and experience here than by saying, firstly, that I regard a trial of this climate as purely experimental in each individual case; secondly, that I never see a suffering invalid at the East without wishing he could have the opportunity to make that experiment.

The Ants' Monday Dinner

Jackson based "The Ants' Monday Dinner" on an experience she had while sitting on a Colorado hillside one afternoon. As she recounted in her essay, she had noticed an ant carrying a caterpillar and had decided to see where the ant was taking its still struggling prey. In her essay, she provided a detailed description of the ant's difficult trip back to its colony. She also, however, included amusing dialogue, which she imagined the ant might have said or thought. This essay first appeared in Jackson's book BITS OF TALK, IN VERSE AND PROSE, FOR YOUNG FOLKS (1876).

How did I know what the ants had for dinner last Monday? Ha, it is odd that I should have known, but I'll tell you how it happened.

I was sitting under a big pine-tree, high up on a high hill-side. The hill-side was more than seven thousand feet above the sea, and that is higher than many mountains which people travel hundreds of miles to look at. But this hill-side was in Colorado, so there was nothing wonderful in being so high up. I had been watching the great mountains with snow on them, and the great forests of pine-trees—-miles and miles of them—-so close together that it looks as if you could lie down on their tops and not fall through; and my eyes were tired with looking at such great, grand things, so many miles off; so I looked down on the ground where I was sitting, and watched the ants which were running about everywhere, as busy and restless as if they had the whole world on their shoulders.

Suddenly I saw, under a tuft of grass, a tiny yellow caterpillar, which seemed to be bounding along in a very strange way. In a second more, I saw an ant seize hold of him and begin to drag him off. The caterpillar was three times as long as the ant, and his body was more than twice as large round as the biggest part of the ant's body.

"Ho! ho! Mr. Ant," said I, "you needn't think you're going to be strong enough to drag that fellow very far."

Why, it was about the same thing as if you or I should drag off a heifer, which was kicking and struggling for dear life all the time; only that the heifer hasn't half so many legs to catch hold of things with as the caterpillar had. Poor caterpillar! how he did try to get away! But the ant never gave him a second's time to take a good grip of anything; and he was cunning enough, too, to drag him on his side, so that he couldn't use his legs very well. Up and down, and under and over stones and sticks; in and out of tufts of grass; up to the very top of the tallest blades, and then down again; over gravel and sand, and across bridges of pine-needles from stone to stone; backward all the way—but for all I could see, just as swiftly as if he were going headforemost—-ran that ant, dragging the caterpillar after him. I watched him very closely, thinking, of course, he must be making for his house. Presently, he darted up the trunk of the pine-tree.

"Dear me!" said I, "ants don't live in trees! What does this mean?"

The bark of the tree was all broken and jagged, and full of seams twenty times as deep as the height of the ant's body. But he didn't mind; down one side and up the other he went. They must have been awful chasms to him; and to the poor caterpillar too, for their sharp edges caught and tore his skin, and doubled him up a dozen ways in a minute. And yet the ant never once stopped or went a bit slower. I had to watch very closely, not to lose sight of him altogether. I began to think that he was merely trying to kill the caterpillar; that, perhaps, he didn't mean to eat him, after all. Perhaps he was merely a gentlemanly sportsman ant, out on a frolic. How did I know but some ants might hunt caterpillars, just as some men hunt deer, for fun, and not at all because they need food? If I had been sure of this, I would have spoiled Mr. Ant's sport for him very soon, you may be sure, and set the poor caterpillar free. But I never heard of an ant's being cruel; and if it were really for dinner for his family that he was working so hard, I thought he ought to be helped, and not hindered. Just then my attention was diverted from him by a sharp cry overhead. I looked up, and there was an enormous hawk, sailing round in circles, with two small birds flying after him, pouncing down on his head, and then darting away, and all the time making shrill cries of fright and hatred. I knew very well what that meant. Mr. Hawk was also out trying to do some marketing for his dinner; and he had his eye on some little birds in their nest; and there were the father and mother birds driving him away. You wouldn't have believed two such little birds could have driven off such a big creature as the hawk, but they did. They seemed to fairly buzz round his head as flies do round a horse's head, and at last he just gave up and flew off so far that he vanished in the blue sky, and the little birds came skimming home again into the wood.

"Well, well," said I, "the little people are stronger than the big ones, after all! Where has my ant gone?"

Sure enough! It hadn't been two minutes that I had been watching the hawk and the birds, but in that two minutes the ant and the caterpillar had disappeared. At last I found them, — where do you think? In a fold of my water-proof cloak, on which I was sitting! The ant had let go of the caterpillar, and was running round and round him, perfectly bewildered; and the caterpillar was too near dead to stir. I shook the fold out, and as soon as the cloth lay straight and smooth, the ant fastened his nippers in the caterpillar again, and started off as fast as ever. I suppose if I could have seen his face, and had understood the language of ants' features, I should have seen plainly written there, "Dear me, what sort of a country was that I tumbled into, so frightfully black and smooth?" By this time the caterpillar had had the breath pretty well knocked out of his body, and was so limp and helpless that the ant was not afraid of his getting away from him. So he stopped a second now and then to rest. Sometimes he would spring on the caterpillar's back, and stretch himself out there; sometimes he would stand still on one side and look at him sharply, keeping on nipper on his head. All the time, though, he was working steadily in one direction; he was headed for home now, I felt very certain. It astonished me very much at first, that none of the ants he met took any notice of him; they all went on their own way, and never took so much as a sniff at the caterpillar. But pretty soon I said to myself, "You stupid woman, not to suppose that ants can be as well behaved as people! When you passed Mr. Jones yesterday, you didn't peep into his market-basket, nor touch the big cabbage he had under his arms."

Presently, the ant dropped the caterpillar, and ran on a few steps—I mean inches——to meet another ant who was coming towards him. They put their heads close together for a second. I could not hear what they said, but I could easily imagine, for they both ran quickly back to the caterpillar, and one took him by the head and the other by the tail, and then they lugged him along finely. It was only a few steps, however, to the ant's house; that was the reason he happened to meet this friend just coming out. The door was a round hole in the ground, about as big as my little finger. Several ants were standing in the door-way, watching these two come up with the caterpillar. They all took hold as soon as the caterpillar was on the door-step, and almost before I knew he was fairly there, they had tumbled him down, heels over head, into the ground, and that was the last I saw of him.

The oddest thing was how the ants came running home from all directions. I don't believe there was any dinner-bell rung, though there might have been one too fine for my ears to hear; but in less than a minute, I had counted thirty-three ants running down that hole. I fancied they looked as hungry as wolves.

I had a great mind to dig down into the hole with a stick, and see what had become of the caterpillar. But I thought it wasn't quite fair to take the roof off a man's house to find out how he cooks his beef for dinner; so I sat still awhile, and wondered whether they would lay him straight on the floor, and all stand in rows each side of him and nibble across, and whether they would leave any for Tuesday; and then I went home to my own dinner.

10

Nelly's Silver Mine

The following excerpt from NELLY'S SILVER MINE comes from the final third of the book, which is the section that deals with silver mining. In the chapters immediately preceding this excerpt, the March family is struggling to make a go of it on their new ranch. Nelly March and her twin brother, Rob, want to help their parents, but they are not sure how until Nelly comes up with the idea of selling eggs and butter to the people in the nearby town of Rosita. It is during one of her trips to Rosita that she becomes involved in silver mining. This excerpt has been edited. Several passages that do not pertain to Nelly's silver mining experiences have been deleted, and the original chapter headings have been omitted.

When Nelly set off on her next trip to Rosita, she wore on her head a man's hat, with a brim so broad you could hardly see her face at all. She had to wear this ever since the summer weather began: the sun is so hot in Colorado that no one can bear it on his head or face in the summer. On Nelly's arm swung her neat white sun-bonnet, tied by its strings, and pinned up in paper. When she reached the last hill before entering the town, she always took off her hat, and hid it in a hollow place she had found in the root of a great pine-tree; then she wore her sun-bonnet into town, and people sometimes said to her:—

"Why, Nelly, how do you keep your sun-bonnet so clean, after this long, dusty walk?"

But Nelly never told her secret. She was afraid some boy might hear it, and go and find the hiding-place of her hat.

There wasn't a boy to be seen when Nelly entered the town this morning. After she had left the butter and eggs for Mrs. Clapp, and had sold the rest of her eggs at another house nearby, she walked slowly down the hill past the hotel. Just below the hotel was a little one-story wooden building, which had a sign up over the door— "Wilhelm Kleesman, Assayer."

While the Marches were staying at the hotel, Nelly had often seen old Mr. Kleesman sitting on the steps of his little house, and smoking a big brown pipe. The bowl of the pipe had carved on it a man's head, with a long, flowing beard. Mr. Kleesman himself had a long, flowing beard, as white as snow, and his face did not look unlike the face on the pipe; and the first time Rob saw him smoking, he had run to call Nelly, saying:—

"Come here, Nell! come quick! There's a man out there smoking, with his own portrait on his pipe."

Mr. March had explained to Nelly and Rob that "Assayer" meant a man who could take a stone and find out whether there were really any silver and gold in it or not. This seemed very wonderful to the children; and, as they looked at the old gentleman sitting on his door-step every

Cover of Nelly's Silver Mine *from the 1935 edition published by Little, Brown and Co., Boston, 1935. Helen Roosevelt Richards, artist.*

evening, smoking, they thought he looked like a magician, or like Aladdin who had the wonderful lamp. Rob said he meant to go and show him some of his stones, and see if there were not silver in some of them; but his father told him that it took a great deal of time and trouble to find out whether a stone had silver in it or not, and that everybody who had it done had to pay Mr. Kleesman three dollars for doing it.

"Whew!" said Rob: "supposing there shouldn't be any silver at all in their stone, what then?"

"They have to pay three dollars all the same," said his father; "and it is much cheaper to find out that way, than it is to go on digging and digging, and spending time and money getting stones out of the earth which are not good for any thing."

After that, Rob and Nelly used to watch the faces of all the men they saw coming out of Mr. Kleesman's office, and try to guess whether their stones had turned out good or not. If the man looked sad and disappointed, Nelly would say:—

"Oh! see that poor man: his hasn't turned out good, I know."

And, whenever some one came out with a quick step and a smiling face, Rob would say:—

"Look! look! Nell. That man's got silver. He's got it: I know he has."

As Nelly walked by Mr. Kleesman's house this morning, she saw lying on the ground a queer little round cup. It was about half as big as a small, old-fashioned teacup; it was made of a rough sort of clay, like that which flower-pots are made of; the outside was white, and the inside was all smooth and shining, and of a most beautiful green color.

"Oh, what a pretty little cup!" thought Nelly, picking it up, and looking at it closely. "I wonder how it came here! Somebody must have lost it; some little girl, I guess. How sorry she will be!"

At that minute, old Mr. Kleesman came to his door. When he saw Nelly looking at the cup, he called out to her:— "Vould you like more as dat? I haf plenty; dey iss goot for little girls."

Mr. Kleesman was a German, and spoke very broken English.

Nelly looked up at him, and said:—

"Thank you, sir. I should like some more very much. They are cunning little cups. I thought somebody had lost this one."

Mr. Kleesman laughed, and stroked his long, white beard with his hand.

"Ach! I throw dem away each day. Little girls come often to mine room for dem: I have vary goot customers in little girls. Come in! come in! you shall have so many that you want." And he led Nelly into a small back room, where, in a corner on the floor, was a great pile of these little cups: some broken ones; some, like the one Nelly had, green on the inside; some brown, some yellow, some dark-red. Nelly was delighted. She knelt down on the floor, and began to look over the pile.

"May I really have all I want?" she said. "Are they not of any use?"

"Only to little girls," said Mr. Kleesman: "sometimes to a boy; but not often a boy; mostly it is for little girls; they are my goot customers."

Nelly picked out six. She did not like to take more, though she would have liked the whole pile. Mr. Kleesman stood watching her. "Vy not you take more as dem?" he said.

"I am afraid there will not be enough for the other little girls," replied Nelly.

Mr. Kleesman laughed and shook till his white beard went up and down.

"Look you here," he said, and pointed behind the door. There was another pile, twice as big as the one which Nelly was examining.

"Oh, my!" said Nelly: "what a lot! I'll take a few more, I guess."

"I gif you myself. You haf too modest," said the old gentleman. And he picked up two big handfuls of the cups, and threw them into Nelly's basket. Then he sprang to a big brick stove which there was in the room, and opened its iron door and looked in. A fiery heat filled the room, as he opened the door.

"Oh!" said Nelly, "I wondered what made it so hot in here. Why do you have a fire in such hot weather?" she said.

"To make mine assays," replied Mr. Kleesman. "I haf made three to-day already. I shall make three more. I haf big fire all day. You can look in if you like. Do you like?"

"Very much," said Nelly. Mr. Kleesman lifted her up on a block of wood, so that her face came directly opposite the door into the furnace. Then he gave her a piece of wood shaped like a shovel, with two round holes in it. He told her to hold this up in front of her face, so to keep off the heat, and then to look through the two holes into the furnace. Nelly did so; and, as soon as she looked into the fiery furnace, she gave a little scream. The fire was one mass of glowing red coals. In the centre, on a stand, stood three little cups, the same size as those she had. In these cups was something which was red hot, and bubbling in little bubbles. "Oh! what is it in the cups?" she cried.

"Silver ore," replied Mr. Kleesman. "It have to be burnt and burnt wiz fire before I can tell if it are good. It are done now. I take out." Then with a long pair of tongs he took out one cup after another, and set them all on an iron block on the table.

Nelly stood on tiptoe, and looked into the little cups. The fiery red color died away very quickly; and there, in the bottom of each cup, was a tiny, little round speck of silver. One was as big as the head of a common-sized pin, and one was a little smaller, and the third one was so small you could but just see it. In fact, if it had been loose on the floor or on a table, you would not have noticed it at all.

"That is not goot for any t'ing," said Mr. Kleesman, pointing to this small one. "I tell the man ven he bring his ore, I think it are no good."

Nelly did not speak; but her face was so full of eager curiosity that Mr. Kleesman said:—

"Now I show you how I tell how much silver there will be in each ton of the ore."

Then he went into the front room, and Nelly followed him. On a table in the window stood a long box; its sides and top were made of glass, set in narrow wooden frames. In this box was a beautiful little pair of brass scales; and in one of these scales was a tiny silver button. One side of this glass box drew up like a sliding door. Mr. Kleesman set his little cups down very carefully on the table;

then he sat down in a chair opposite the glass box, and told Nelly to come and stand close to him.

"Now I weigh," he said, and pulled up the sliding side of the glass box; then with a very fine pair of pincers he took up one of the little buttons which had come out of the furnace, and laid it in the empty scale.

"See which are the heaviest," he said to Nelly.

Nelly strained her eyes; but she could hardly see that one scale was heavier than the other. "They are alike," said Nelly. Mr. Kleesman laughed.

"Ah, no! but they are not," he said. "Look! here it is written." And he pointed to a little needle which was fastened on the upright bar from which the scales swung. This needle was balanced so that the very smallest possible weight would make it move one way or the other, and point to figures printed on a scale behind it,—just as you have seen figures on the scales the cooks weigh sugar and butter on in the kitchen. Mr. Kleesman took off the glasses he was wearing, and put on another pair. "These are my best eyes," he said, "to read the small figures with." Then he peered a few minutes at the needle; then he shut down the glass slide, and watched it through the glass.

"Even my breath would make that it did not swing true," he said.

Presently he pushed up the slide, and took out the little button with his pincers, and put it up on a bar above the scales, where there were as many as a dozen more of the little buttons, all arranged in a row,—some larger, some smaller. Then he wrote a few words in a little book.

"There," he said, "I haf good news for two men, and bad news for one man,—the man who haf the little button; his mine are not goot. The other two can make twelve dollars of silver from one ton of ore."

By this time Nelly looked so hopelessly puzzled, that the old gentleman laughed, and said:—

"You haf not understand: is that so?"

"Oh, no, sir!" said Nelly: "I have not understood at all. Could I understand?"

"Ach, yes! it is so simple, so simple; the smallest child shall understand, if I show him. Stay you here till afternoon, and I show you from beginning," said Mr. Kleesman, "I make two more assays this afternoon."

"Thank you, sir," replied Nelly: "I should like to stay very much; but my brother is waiting for me. I must hurry home. Some other day, if you will let me, I will come. May I bring my brother?"

"Is he goot like you; not to touch, and not ask the questions that are foolish?" said Mr. Kleesman.

Nelly colored. She was afraid Rob would not be able to keep as quiet as she had, or to refrain from touching things. Yet she wanted to have him see the curious sight.

"I think he will not touch any thing if you ask him not to; and I will try to keep him very still," said Nelly.

"Vary goot: he may come. Little one, it will be to me pleasure to show you all. You are like German child, not like American child," replied Mr. Kleesman, whose heart warmed towards Nelly more and more the longer he watched her quiet ways and her thoughtful face.

It seemed very long to Rob and Nelly before the day came round to go up to Rosita again. It was only two days; but it seemed as much as a week to them both. That is one of the queerest things in this life, I think, that time can seem both so much longer and so much shorter than it really is. Haven't you known Saturday afternoons that didn't seem one bit more than a minute long? I have; and I remember just as well all about them, as if it were only this very last Saturday.

At last, the day came. It was Friday, and a lovely, bright day. Mr. March had said that Rob might go too; and both the children were awake long before light, in their impatience to be off.

"It would do just as well if we got up there early enough to be all through with selling things, and get in to Mr. Kleesman's before nine o'clock: wouldn't it, Nell?" said Rob.

"Why, yes," said Nelly, "of course it would. That's splendid. Let's get right up now. It's beginning to be light." When Mrs. March heard their feet pattering about, she called from her room:— "What in the world are you about, children?"

"Getting up, mamma," answered Nelly. "We're going up to town real early, so as to get out of the way of the boys, and have a good long time at Mr. Kleesman's. It takes about three hours to do what he does to the ore. Can't we go?"

"I have no objection," replied Mrs. March; "but you must have some breakfast. I will get right up."

"Oh, no! no! please, dear mamma, don't!" cried Nelly. "It's only four o'clock, by the clock downstairs: I've just been down. We can get plenty to eat without you. There is beautiful cream in the pantry; and a whole lot of cold potatoes."

Mrs. March laughed, and said:— "I don't think cold potatoes are a very good breakfast."

"Why, mamma! mamma!" cried Rob, "cold potatoes are splendid. I like them best cold, with lots of salt. Please don't you get up."

Mrs. March was very sleepy; so she turned over in bed, and went sound to sleep. When Nelly was dressed, she peeped cautiously in at the door of her mother's room, which stood open.

"They're both sound asleep, Rob," she whispered: "let's take off our shoes."

"What fun!" whispered Rob; and the two children stole downstairs in their stocking-feet, like two little thieves; then they drank a good tumbler of cream, and ate the cold potatoes with salt, and some nice brown bread, and butter.

As the children went out of the house, the sky in the east was just beginning to be bright red. The sun was not up; but it was very light, and Pike's Peak shone against the red sky like a great mountain of alabaster. The peaks of the mountains in the west were rosy red; all their tops were covered with snow, and in the red light they looked like jewels.

"Oh, Rob, look! look!" cried Nelly: "isn't it perfectly lovely! Let's always come early like this."

Rob looked at the mountains and the sky.

"Yes, 'twould be pretty if 'twould stay so," he said; "but 'twon't last a minute."

Even while he spoke, the red color faded; the mountains began to look blue; and, in a minute more, up came the sun over the Rosita hills, and flooded the whole valley with a yellow light. All along the sides of the road were beautiful flowers,—blue, pink, white, yellow, and red. It had rained in the night; and every flower was shining with rain-drops, and as bright as if it had just been painted.

The children had a droll time going to people's houses so early. Nobody was up. At Mrs. Glapp's, they had to pound and pound, before they could wake anybody. Then Mr. Clapp put his head out of a window to see what had happened.

"Goodness!" he said: "here are the children with the butter. How did they ever get up here so early." And he ran down to open the door. "Ask them to stay to breakfast," said Mrs. Clapp. "The poor little things must be faint."

Nelly and Rob thanked Mr. Clapp, but said they could not stop.

"We had a splendid breakfast at home," said Rob, triumphantly.

When Mr. Clapp went back to his room, he said to his wife:—

"Poor little things, indeed! You wouldn't have called them so, if you'd seen them. Their eyes shone like diamonds, and their cheeks were just like roses; and they looked as full of frolic as kittens. I declare I do envy March those children. That Nelly's going to make a most beautiful woman."

Rob and Nelly reached Mr. Kleesman's door at eight o'clock. His curtains were down: no sign of life about the place.

"I say, Nell, aren't the Rosita people lazy!" exclaimed Rob. "What'll we do now?"

"Sit down here on the step and wait," said Nelly. "He always comes out here, the first thing, and looks off down into the valley, and at the mountains. I used to see him when we were at the hotel."

How long it seemed before they heard steps inside the house; and then how much longer still before the door opened! When Mr. Kleesman saw the little figures sitting on his door-step, he started.

"Ach, my soul!" he exclaimed: "it is the little one. Good morning! good morning!" And he stooped over and kissed Nelly's forehead.

"This is my brother, sir," said Nelly. "We are all done with our work, and have come to see you make the assay. You said you could show us."

"Ach! ach!" cried the old gentleman; and he looked very sorry. "It is one tousand of pities: it cannot be that I show you to-day. My chimney he did do smoke; and a man will come now this hour to take out my furnace the flue. It must be made new. Not for some day I make the assay more."

Nelly and Rob looked straight in his face without speaking: they were too disappointed to say one word. Kind old Mr. Kleesman was very sorry for them.

"You shall again come: I will show the very first day," he said.

"Thank you, sir," said Nelly. "We always come into town Tuesdays and Fridays. We can come to your house any time." And she took hold of Rob's hand, and began to go down the steps.

"Vait! vait!" exclaimed Mr. Kleesman: "come in, and I show you some picture of Malacca. I did live many years in Malacca." Rob bounded at these words. His whole face lighted up.

"Oh, thank you! thank you!" he said: "that is what I like best in all the world."

"Vat is dat you like best in all the vorld: Malacca?" said the old gentleman. "And vy like you Malacca?"

Rob looked confused. Nelly came to his rescue.

"He doesn't mean that he likes Malacca, sir," she said: "only that he likes to hear about strange countries,—any countries."

"Ach!" said Mr. Kleesman: "I see. He vill be one explorer."

"Indeed I will that!" said Rob. "Just as soon as I'm a man." I'm going all round this world."

Mr. Kleesman had lived ten years in Malacca. He had been in charge of tin mines there. He was an artist too, this queer old gentleman; and he had painted a great many small pictures of things and places he saw there. These he kept in an old leather portfolio, on a shelf above his bed. This portfolio he now took down, and spread the pictures out on the bed, for Rob and Nelly to look at. There was a picture of the house he lived in while he was in Malacca. It was built of bamboo sticks and rattan, and looked like a little toy house. There was a picture of one of the queer boats a great many of the Malay people live in. Think of that: live in a boat all the time, and never have a house on land at all. These boats are about twenty feet long, and quite narrow; at one end they have a fireplace, and at the other end their bedroom. The bedroom is nothing but a mat spread over four poles; and under this mat the whole family sits by day and sleeps by night. They move about from river to river, and live on fish, and on wild roots which they dig on the banks of the rivers.

"My servant lif in that boat," said Mr. Kleesman. "He take wife, and go lif in a boat. His name is Jinghi. I write it for you in Malay."

Then Mr. Kleesman wrote on a piece of paper some very queer characters, which Nelly said looked just like the letters on tea-chests.

While they were talking, there came in a man in rough clothes, a miner, carrying a small bag of stout canvas. He opened it, and took out a handful of stones, of a very dark color, almost black.

"Would you dig where you found that?" he said, holding out the stones to Mr. Kleesman.

Mr. Kleesman took them in his hand, looked at them attentively, and said:—

"Yes, that is goot mineral. There might be mine vere dat mineral is on top. We haf proverb in our country, 'No mine is not wort not'ing unless he haf black hat on his head.'"

The man put his stones back in his bag, nodded his head, and went out, saying:— "I reckon we'll buy that claim. I'll let you know."

A small piece of the stone had fallen on the floor. Nelly eyed it like a hawk. She was trying to remember where she had seen stones just like it. She knew she had seen them somewhere: she recollected thinking at the time how very black the stones were. She picked up the little piece of stone, and asked Mr. Kleesman if it were good for anything.

"Oh, no for not'ing," he said, and turned back to the pictures. Nelly's interest in the pictures had grown suddenly very small. The little black stone had set her to thinking. She put it in her pocket, and told Rob it was time to go home.

"Ven vill you again come," said Mr. Kleesman.

"Next Tuesday," replied Nelly. "That is our day."

"Perhaps it vill be done den: perhaps not: cannot tell. But ven is done, I show you all how I make mine assay," said Mr. Kleesman, and kissed Nelly again as he bade them goodby. All the way home Nelly was thinking hard about the black stones.

After Nelly went to bed that night, she lay awake a long time, still thinking about the black stones. She had put the little piece of stone on the bureau, and while she was undressing she hardly took her eyes off it. She recollected just how the place looked where she saw them. It was a ravine: there were piles of stones at the bottom of the ravine, and a good many scattered all along the sides. There were pine-trees and bushes too: it was quite a shady place.

"I should know it in a minute, if I saw it again," said Nelly to herself; "but where, oh! where was it!"

At last, all in one second, it flashed into her mind. It was one day when she had started for Rosita later than usual, and had thought she would take a short cut across the hills; but she had found it anything but a short cut. As soon as she had climbed one hill she found another rising directly before her, and, between the two a great ravine, down to the very bottom of which she must go before she could climb the other hill. She had crossed several of these ravines,—she did not remember how many,—and had come out at last on the top of the highest of all the hills above the town: a hill so steep that she had always wondered how the cows could keep on their feet when they were grazing high up on it. It was in one of these ravines that she had seen the black stones; but in which one she could not be sure. Neither could she recollect exactly where she had left the road and struck out to cross the hills.

"I might walk and walk all day," thought Nelly, "and never find it. How shall I ever manage?"

Fortune favored Nelly. The very next day, their neighbor, Billy, came to the house to ask if Mrs. March could spare Nelly to go and stay two days with Lucinda, his wife, while he was away. He had an excellent chance to make some money by taking a party of gentlemen across the valley and up into one of the passes in the range, where they were going to fish. He would be at home the second night: Nelly need stay only over one night. Lucinda was not well, and Billy did not like to leave her alone.

Mrs. March said, "Certainly: Nelly could go."

As soon as she told Nelly of the plan, Nelly's heart seemed to leap in her bosom with the thought:— "Now that's just the chance for me to look for the stones."

She set off very early, and reached Lucinda's house before eight o'clock. After she had unpacked her bag, and arranged all her things in the little room where she was to sleep, she asked Lucinda if there were anything she could do to help her.

Lucinda was quilting a big bedquilt, which was stretched out on chairs and long wooden bars, and took up so much of the room in the kitchen it was hard to get about.

"Mercy, no child!" said Lucinda. "I hain't got nothin' to do but this quilt, an' I expect you ain't much of a hand at quiltin'. 'Twan't my notion to have ye come,—not but what I'm always glad to see ye; ye know that,—but I wan't afraid to be alone. But Billy he's took it into his head 'tain't safe for me to be alone here nights. Now if there's anything ye want to do, ye jest go'n' do it."

"Would it make any difference to you if were gone all day, so I am here to sleep?" said Nelly.

"Why, no," replied Lucinda; "not a bit. Did ye want to go into the town?"

"No," said Nelly; "but I wanted to find a place I saw once, on the way there. It was a real deep place, almost sunk down in the ground, full of pines and bushes: a real pretty place. But it wasn't on the road. I don't know's I can find it; but I'd like to."

"All right," said Lucinda: "you go off. I'll give ye some lunch in case ye get hungry. Ye won't be lonesome, will ye, without Rob?"

"Oh, no!" said Nelly: "I like to be all alone outdoors."

Then she bade Lucinda good-by, and set off. For a half mile or so, she walked in the road toward Rosita. She recollected that she had passed Lucinda's before she turned off from the road. But the more she tried to remember the precise spot where she had turned off the more confused she became. At last she sprang out of the road, on the left hand side, and began running as fast as she could.

"I may as well strike off in one place as another," she thought, "since I can't remember. It cannot be very far from here."

She climbed one steep hill, and ran down into the ravine beyond it; then another hill, and another ravine,—no black stones. The sun was by this time high, and very hot. Nelly had done some severe climbing.

"On the top of the next hill I'll eat my lunch," she thought.

The next hill was the steepest one yet. How Nelly did puff and pant before she reached the top; and when she reached it, there was not a single tree big enough to shade her!

"Oh, dear!" said Nelly; and looked up and down the ravine, to see if she could spy any shade anywhere. A long way off to the north, she saw a little clump of pines and oaks. She walked slowly in that direction, keeping her foothold with difficulty in the rolling gravel on the steep side of the hill. Just as she reached the first oak-brush, her foot slipped, and she clutched hard at the bush to save herself: the bush gave way, and she rolled down, bush and all, to the very bottom of the ravine. Luckily, it was soft, sandy gravel all the way, and she was not in the least hurt: only very dirty and a good deal frightened.

"I'll walk along now at the bottom, where it is level," said Nelly, "and not climb up till I come to where the trees are." There had been at some time or other a little stream in this ravine, and it was in the stony bed of it that Nelly was walking. She looked very carefully at the stones. They were all light gray or reddish colored: not a black one among them. She had in her pocket the little piece Mr. Kleesman had given her: she took it out, and looked at it again. It was totally unlike all the stones she saw about her.

"Oh, dear!" sighed Nelly: "I expect I won't find it to-day. I'll come again to-morrow. At any rate I'll go to that nice, shady place to eat my lunch."

It was further than she thought. In Colorado, every thing looks a great deal nearer to you than it really is: the air is so thin and light that mountains twenty miles away look as if they were not more than three or four; and there are a great many funny stories of the mistakes into which travellers are led by this peculiarity of the air. They set off before breakfast, perhaps, to walk to a hill which looks only a little way off; and, after they have walked an hour or two, there stands the hill, still seeming just as far off as ever. One of the funniest stories is of a man who had been cheated in this way so often that at last he didn't believe his eyes any longer as to whether a distance were long or short; and one day he was found taking off his shoes and stockings to wade through a little ditch that anybody could easily step over.

"Why, man alive!" said the people who stood by, "what are you about? You don't need to wade a little ditch like that! Step across it."

"Ha!" said he, "you needn't try to fool me anymore. I expect that ditch is ten feet wide."

Nelly walked on and on in the narrow stony bed of the dried-up stream. The stones hurt her feet, but it was easier walking than on the rolling gravel of the steep sides above. She stopped thinking about the black stones. She was so hot and tired and hungry, all she thought of was getting to the trees to sit down. At last she reached the place just below them. They were much higher upon the hillside than she had supposed. She stood looking up at them.

"I expect I'll tumble before I get up there," she thought. It looked about as steep as the side of the roof to a house. But the shade was so cool and inviting that Nelly thought it worth trying for. Halfway up her feet slipped, and down she came on her knees. She scrambled up; and, as she looked down, what should she see, in the place where her knees had pressed into the gravel, but a bit of the black stone! At first she thought it was the very piece she had had in her pocket; but she felt in her pocket, and there was her own piece all safe. She took it out, held the two together, looked at them, turned them over and over: yes! the stones were really, exactly the same color! Now she was so excited that she forgot all about the heat, and all about her hunger.

"This must be the very ravine!" she said, and began to look eagerly about her for more of the stones. Not another bit could she find! In her eager search, she did not observe that she was slowly working down the hill, till suddenly she found herself again at the bottom of the ravine, in the dried bed of the brook. Then she stood still, and looked around her, considering what to do. At last she decided to walk on up the ravine.

"The big pile of them was right in such a deep place as this," thought Nelly: "I guess it's farther up."

It was very hard walking, and Nelly was beginning to grow tired and discouraged again, when lo! right at her feet, in among the gray stones and the red ones, lay a small black one. She picked it up: it was of the same kind. A few steps farther on, another, and another: she began to stoop fast, picking them up, one by one. She had one hand full: then she looked ahead and, only a little farther on, there she saw the very place she recollected so well,—the ravine full of bushes, and low pine-trees, and piles of stones among them. She had found it! Can you imagine how Nelly felt? You see she believed that it was just the same thing as if she had found a great sum of money. How would you feel if you should suddenly find at your feet thousands and thousands of dollars, if your father and mother were very poor, and needed money very much? I think you would feel just as Nelly did. She sat straight down on the ground, and looked at the stones, and felt as if she should cry,—she was so glad! Then the thought came into her mind:—

"Perhaps this land belongs to somebody who won't sell it. Perhaps he knows there is a mine here!" She looked all about, but she could not see any stakes set up to show that it was owned by any-one: so she hoped it was not.

Now that the excitement of the search was over, she began to feel very hungry again, and ate her lunch with a great relish. The thoughtful Lucinda had put in the basket a small bottle of milk. Nelly thought she had never tasted anything so good in her life as that milk. When you are very thirsty, milk tastes much better than water. After Nelly had eaten her lunch, she filled her basket with the black stones, and set off for home. Presently she began to wonder if she could find her way back again to the spot.

"That would be too dreadful," thought she: "to lose it, now I've just found it." Then she recollected how, in the story of Hop o' My Thumb, it said that when he was carried off into the forest he slyly dropped beans all along the way, to mark the path, and thus found his way back, very easily by means of them. So she resolved to walk along in the bed of the stream, till it was time to climb up and strike off toward Lucinda's, and then to drop red stones all along the way she went, till she reached the beaten road. She took up the skirt of her gown in front, and filled it full with little red stones. Then she trudged along with as light a heart as ever any little girl had, scattering the stones along the way, like a farmer planting corn.

When she reached the road, she was surprised to see that she had come out the other side of Lucinda's house, full quarter of a mile nearer home.

"Now this isn't anywhere near where I left the road before," she said. "How I'll ever tell the place?"

At first she thought she would put a bush up in the crotch of a little pine-tree that stood just there.

"No, that won't do," she said: "the wind might blow it out."

Then she thought she would stick the bush in the sand; but she feared some horse or cow might munch it and pull it up. At last she decided to break down a small bough of the pine-tree, and leave it hanging.

"We can't make a mistake, then, possibly," she thought.

When she reached the house, Lucinda had cleared the bedquilt all away, and had the table set for supper, though it was only half-past four o'clock. Nelly was not hungry. It seemed to her only a few minutes since she ate her lunch.

"Did you find the place, Nelly?" said Lucinda.

"Yes," said Nelly.

"Was it as pretty as it was before?" Lucinda asked.

"Oh, yes!" said Nelly; "but it was awful steep getting down it. I kept tumbling down."

"Well, you're the curiousest child ever was!" exclaimed Lucinda. "Anybody'd think you got walkin' enough in a week without trampin' off this way."

Nelly did not reply. She felt a little guilty at letting Lucinda think it was only to find a pretty place she had gone; but she was sure it would not be best to tell anybody about the black stones till she had told her father. She had hid them all in a pile near the pine-tree whose branch she had broken down; and she meant to pick them up on her way home the next night. In the morning it looked to Nelly as if it never would be night, she was in such a hurry to see her father.

"Oh, Lucinda," she said, "do give me something to do! I don't want to go off to-day. I want to stay with you." So Lucinda gave her some brown towels to hem, and also let her snap the chalked cord with which she marked out the pattern on her quilt; and, by help of these two occupations, Nelly contrived to get through the day, till four o'clock, when she set out for home. As good luck would have it, when she was within quarter of a mile from home she saw her father at work in the field. She jumped over the fence and ran to him.

"Papa! papa!" she said, breathless: "look here!" And she held up her basket of black stones. "This is the kind of stone that comes where the silver is. There is a mine underneath it always: Mr. Kleesman said so. And I've found a mine: I'll show you where it is." Mr. March' laughed very heartily.

"Why, my dear little girl!" he said, "what ever put such an idea into your head? I don't believe those stones are good for anything."

Nelly set down her basket, and pulled her pocket-handkerchief out of her pocket: the little piece of black stone she had got from Mr. Kleesman was tied firm in one corner.

"Look at that papa," she said, "and see if the stones in the basket are not just like it." Then she told her father all about the man's coming into the assayer's office with a bag of stones like that one, and what Mr. Kleesman said to him.

"Don't you see, papa," she said, vehemently, "that it must be a mine? Why, there are piles of it: it has all slipped down into the bottom of this steep place; there used to be a brook down there. I know it's a mine, papa! And if I found it, it's ours: isn't it?"

Nelly's cheeks were red, and her words came so fast they almost choked her.

"Nelly, dear," said her father, "don't you recollect that once before you thought you had found silver ore, you and Rob, up in the Ute Pass?"

"Oh, papa, that was quite different. That was when we were little things. Papa, I know this is a mine. If you'd heard what Mr. Kleesman said, you'd think so too. He said in his country they had a proverb, that no mine was good for anything unless it had a black hat on its head; and that meant that there were always black stones on top like this." Mr. March tuned the little bit of black stone over and over, and examined it carefully.

"I do not know much about minerals," he said. "I think I never saw a stone like this."

"Nor I either, papa," exclaimed Nelly: "except in this one place. I know it's a mine, and I'll give it to you all for your own. It's mine, isn't it, if I found it?"

"Yes, dear, it's yours, unless somebody else had found it before you."

"I don't believe anybody had," said Nelly; "for there weren't any stakes stuck down anywhere near; and all the claims have stakes stuck down round them. Oh, papa! isn't it splendid! now we can have all the money we want."

Mr. March smiled half sadly.

"My dear little daughter," he said, "there are a great many more people who have lost all the money they had in the world trying to get money out of a mine, than there are who have made fortunes in that way. You must not get so excited. Even if there is a mine in the place where you found these stones, I don't think I have money enough to open it and take out the ore. But I will show these stones to Mr. Scholfield. He knows a great deal about mines."

"Oh, do! do! papa," exclaimed Nelly. "I know it's a mine."

"I am going down there to-night," said Mr. March. "I will carry your stones, and see what he says. In the mean time, we will not say anything about it to anybody. You and papa will just have a little secret."

When Nelly kissed her father for good-night, she nodded at him with a meaning glance, and he returned the nod with an equally meaning one.

"What are you two plotting?" cried Mrs. March. "I see mischief in both your eyes."

"Oh, it's a little secret we have, Nelly and I," said Mr. March. "It won't last long: we'll tell you tomorrow."

It turned out that Mrs. March did not have to wait till the next day before learning the secret. Mr. March got home about midnight from Mr. Scholfield's. Mrs. March had been sound asleep for two hours: the sound of Mr. March's steps wakened her.

"Is that you, Robert?" she called.

"Yes," he said. There was something in the tone of his voice which was so strange that it roused her instantly. She sat up straight in bed and exclaimed:—

"What is the matter?"

"Nothing," said Mr. March.

"Nonsense!" said Mrs. March: "you can't deceive me. Something has happened. Come in here this minute and tell me what it is."

Then Mr. March told her the whole story. He had taken Nelly's stones to Mr. Scholfield, who had said immediately that there was without doubt a mine in the place where that mineral was found; and, when Mr. March had told him as nearly as he could from Nelly's description where the spot was, he had said that no mines had yet been discovered very near that place, and no claims were staked out.

"Scholfield says we must go immediately and stake out our claim. He'll go shares with me in digging; and at any rate will see what's there," said Mr. March.

"Do you believe in it yourself, Robert?" asked Mrs. March. She was much afraid of new schemes for making money.

"Why, I can't say I'm very enthusiastic about it," replied Mr. March; "but then I don't know any thing about mines, you see. Scholfield was near wild over it. He says we've got silver there sure."

"Will you have to find money to begin with?" asked Mrs. March, anxiously.

"Well, Sarah, considering that we haven't got any money, I don't see how I can: do you?" laughed Mr. March. "But Scholfield says that if I will give him a third of the mine, he'll take another man in, and they two'll pay for the working it at first. That seems very fair: doesn't it?"

"I don't know," said Mrs. March. "If the mine really does turn out to be very valuable, it is giving him a good deal."

"That is true," replied Mr. March. "But, on the other hand, perhaps it is not worth any thing; and, in that case, Scholfield has the worst of the bargain. He says, though, he can tell very soon. He has been in mining a good deal; and he can make his own assays with the blow-pipe. We're to start very early in the morning, and take Nelly along to show us the way. The dear child was nearly beside herself last night."

"So that was your secret: was it?" said Mrs. March.

"Yes, and a very hard one it was for the child to keep too," said Mr. March. "She was half crazy to tell Rob."

"You'll take him along too: won't you?" asked Mrs. March.

"Oh, yes," said Mr. March: "no more secrets now; that is, not in this house. We won't have it talked round, if we can help it. Scholfield says that the minute it is known we've found silver there, those ravines will just swarm with men prospecting for more claims."

The next day, Mr. March and Mr. Scholfield and Rob and Nelly set out immediately after breakfast for the ravine. They stopped at Billy's house and took him with them. Mr. Scholfield had said to Mr. March, as they walked along;—

"If Billy'll go in with us, I'd rather have him than any man I know about here. He's as honest's daylight; I don't think he's doing much this summer; I think he'll go to work digging right away."

Wasn't Nelly a proud little girl as she walked ahead of the party? She kept hold of Rob's hand, and every now and then they would run so fast that the older people had to run, too, to keep up with them.

"How do you know the way so well, Nelly?" said Mr. Scholfield.

Nelly laughed.

"If you watch closely, you can see what I tell by," she said. "It's in plain sight."

"Yes, plain sight! plain sight!" shouted Rob, to whom Nelly had pointed out the little red stones. "It's out of a story."

Mr. Scholfield and Mr. March and Billy all looked around, perplexed; but they could see nothing.

"Oh, tell us the secret, Guide," said Mr. March. "We are stupid: we can't find it out." Then Nelly told him; and as soon as she pointed to the red stones they wondered very much that they had not noticed them before.

It seemed a very short way to the ravine, this time. Nelly had reached it before she thought of its being near.

"Why, here it is," she said; "I didn't think we were half way there."

Then she and Rob sat on the ground and watched the others. Rob was very quiet. He was a good deal overawed at the idea of a real silver mine all for their own.

"Do you suppose it's right here, right under our feet, Nell?" said he, stamping his foot on the ground.

"I dare say," said Nelly. "Perhaps it is all over round here: some of them are as big as a mile."

"I wonder if they'll let us go down as often as we want to," said Rob. "They'll have to, won't they, if it's our own mine?"

"That'll be for papa to say," answered Nelly, decidedly. "I've given it to him. It's his mine."

While the children were thus building their innocent aircastles in a small way, the brains of the older people were building no less actively, and on a larger scale. Both Billy and Mr. Scholfield were much excited. Billy ran from spot to spot, now hammering a stone in two with his hammer, now digging fiercely into the ground with his pick-axe. Mr. Scholfield went about picking up the black stones, and piling them together, till he had quite a monument of them.

"I declare," he said at last, "it beats me that this place hasn't ever been found before, much's this country's been prospected over and over. I don't know what to make of it. But there isn't a sign of a claim here for miles: I know that."

"Will, I'll tell yer what I'm a thinkin'," said Billy. "I'm a thinkin' that's fur back's them fust prospectin' days there was a creek in here; 'n' that's the reason there didn't nobody look here. I've heern it said hundreds o'times in town thet there wan't no use lookin' along these ridges; they'd all been looked over thorough, 'n' there wan't nothin' in 'em. But we've struck a silver mine, sure: I hain't any doubt of it. Let's name her 'The Little Nelly.'"

Mr. March's face grew red. He did not like the idea of having a mine called after Nelly; but he did not want to hurt Billy's feelings. Before he could speak, Mr. Scholfield cried out:—

"Good for you, Billy! That's what we'll call it! That's a name to bring good luck." 'The Little Nelly!' and may she turn out not so 'little,' after all; and the first bucketful of ore we draw up, Nelly, we'll drink your health, and christen the mine."

Nelly did not quite understand what all this meant. "Did you mean that I am to name the mine, sir?" she said.

"No," said Mr. Scholfield: "we meant that we were going to name it for you, by your name. But you can name it, if you like. That would be luckier still. Don't you like to have it called by your name?"

Nelly hesitated.

"I think I would rather not have it named after me," she said: "some of the mines have such dreadful names. But I know a name I think would be a real pretty name."

"What's that," said her father.

"The Good Luck," said Nelly.

Billy clapped his knee hard with his hand.

"By jingo!" said he, "that's the best name ever was given to a mine yet. 'The Good Luck' it shall be; and good luck it was to you, Nelly, the day you struck it. Old Pine he said, one day last spring, mebbe you'd find a mine, when I was a tellin' him how you'n' Rob was allers looking' for one."

"But I wasn't looking for this, Billy," said Nelly. "I gave up looking for one a long time ago, when we began to sell the eggs. It was just an accident that I happened to remember the black stones in here."

"That's the way some of the best mines have been found," said Mr. Scholfield: "just by sheer accident. There was a man I knew, in California, had his mule run away from him one day: it was somewhere in that Tuolomne region; and if that mule didn't run straight down into a gulch that was just washed full of free gold,— and the fellow had been walking in it some time before he noticed it! There's a heap o' luck in this world."

"Yes," said Mr. March, "there's a great deal of luck; but there is a great deal which is set down to luck which isn't luck. Now, if my little girl here hadn't had the good-will and the energy to try to earn some money for her mother and me, she wouldn't have been searching for a short cut to Rosita over these hills, and would never have found this mine."

"That's so," said Mr. Scholfield, looking admiringly at Nelly. "She's a most uncommon girl, that Nelly of yours. I think we ought to call the mine after her: it's hers."

"No," said Mr. March: "I like her name for it best. Let us call it 'The Good Luck.'"

Mrs. March was watching for her husband and children when they came down the lane. She had been much more excited about the silver mine than she had confessed to Mr. March. All day long she had been unable to keep it out of her mind. The prospect was too tempting. "Why should it not have happened to us, as well as to so many people," she thought. "Oh! if we only could have just money enough to give Rob and Nelly a good education, I would not ask for any thing more. And, even if this is not very much of a mine, it might give us money enough for that." With such hopes and imaginations as these Mrs. March's mind had been full all day long; and, when she saw Mr. March and Rob and Nelly coming toward the house, she felt almost afraid to see them, lest she should see disappointment written on their faces.

Not at all. Rob and Nelly came bounding on ahead, and, as they drew near the door, they shouted out:— "The Good Luck! The Good Luck! It is named 'The Good Luck.'"

"They wanted to call it 'The Little Nelly,' but Nelly wouldn't," said Rob. "I don't see why. If I'd found it, I'd have called it 'The

Rob,' I know. They didn't ask me to let them call it for me. If they had, they might and welcome."

"It is really a mine, then?" said Mrs. March, looking at her husband.

"Yes, Sarah, I think it is," he replied. "If Scholfield and Billy know,—and they seem to be very sure,—there is good promise of silver there; and Nelly herself has named it 'The Good Luck.'"

"Oh, Nelly! did you, really?" exclaimed Mrs. March. "You dear child!" And she threw both arms around Nelly, and gave her a great hug. "That's a lovely name. I do believe it will bring luck."

"I didn't want it named after me" said Nelly. "It isn't as if it was a live thing—"

"Subjunctive mood, dear! 'as if it were,'" interrupted Mrs. March.

"As if it were," repeated Nelly, looking confused. "I wish they'd left the subjunctive mood out of the grammar. I shan't ever learn it! It isn't as if it were a live thing, like a baby or a kitten. I wouldn't mind having such things called after me, but some of the mines have the awfullest names, mamma: real wicked names, that I shouldn't dare to say."

"Well, they'll call it after you, anyhow, Nell," cried Rob. "Billy said so, coming home."

"They won't either," said Nelly, "when it was my own mine, only I gave it to papa, and I asked them not to; I think it would be real mean."

"Oh, I don't mean Mr. Scholfield and Billy," said Rob: "they called it 'The Good Luck' as soon as you said so; but the men round town. They'll hear it was you found it; and they'll call it 'The Nelly,' always: you see if they don't."

"Rob, don't tease your sister so," said Mrs. March.

"Why, does that tease you, Nell?" asked Rob, pretending to be very innocent. "I was only telling you what Billy said."

"I don't believe it, anyway," said Nelly: "do you, papa?"

"No, replied Mr. March. "I do not see why they should give it any other name than the one the owners give it."

"Well, you'll see," said Rob. "There are ever so many mines that go by two or three different names. There's one way off in the north somewhere, where Billy used to haul ore, is called 'Bobtail,' some of the time, and 'Miss Lucy,' some of the time. They tried to change 'Bobtail' into 'Miss Lucy,' and they couldn't."

"Couldn't!" exclaimed Nelly: "what do you mean by that?"

"Why, the people wouldn't," said Rob, saucily: "that's all."

"That's all about a great many things in this world, Rob," laughed his mother. "'Couldn't' is very apt to be only another word for 'wouldn't' with a little boy I know." Rob laughed, and left off teasing Nelly about the name of her mine.

Billy went to work the very next day at "The Good Luck." First, he put up a little hut, which looked more like an Indian wigwam than anything else. This was for him and Mr. Scholfield to sleep in.

"We can't take time to go home nights till we get this thing started," said Billy. "If we've got ore here, the sooner we get some on't out the better; an' if we hain't got ore here, the sooner we find that out the better."

All day long, day after day, Billy and Mr. Scholfield dug, till they had a big hole, as deep as a well, dug in the ground. Then they put a windlass at the top, with a long rope fastened to it, and a bucket on the end of the rope. This bucket they lowered down into the hole, just as you lower a water bucket down into a well; then they filled it full of the stones which they thought had silver in them, and then turned the windlass and drew it up.

Mr. Scholfield pounded some of these stones very fine, and melted it with his blow-pipe, and got quite big buttons of silver out of it. He gave some of these to Mr. March. When he showed these to Nelly, she exclaimed:—

"Oh! these are a great deal bigger than any I saw in Mr. Kleesman's office. Our mine must be a good one."

Mr. Scholfield was in great glee. He made the most extravagant statements, and talked very foolishly about the mine: said he would not take half a million of dollars for his third of it; and so

on, till old, experi-enced miners shook their heads and said he was
crazy. But, when they saw the round buttons of shining silver which
he had extracted from the stones, they stopped shaking their heads,
and thought perhaps he was right. The fame of "The Good Luck"
spread all over town; and, as Billy had said there would be, there
were many who persisted in calling the mine "The Nelly." Almost
everybody in Rosita knew Nelly by sight by this time; and it gave
the mine much greater interest in their eyes that it had been found
by this good, industrious little girl, whom everybody liked.
Whenever Nelly went to town now, people asked her about her
mine. She always answered:—

"It isn't my mine: it is my papa's."

"But you found it," they would say.

"I found the black hat it wore on its head," was Nelly's usual
reply: "that is all. Mr. Scholfield and Billy found the silver."

It happened that it was nearly three weeks before Rob and
Nelly went to Mr. Kleesman's house again. They had now a new
interest, which made them hurry through with all they had to do
in Rosita, so as to have time on their way home to stop at "The
Good Luck," and watch Billy and Mr. Scholfield at work. It was
an endless delight to them to see the windlass wind, wind, wind,
and watch the heavy bucket of stone slowly coming up to the
mouth of the hole. Then Billy would let Rob take the bucket and
empty it on the pile of shining gray ore which grew higher and
higher every day. Sometimes the children stayed here so late that it
was after dark when they reached home; and at last Mrs. March
told them that they must not go to the mine every time they went
to Rosita: it made their walk too long. She said they might go only
every other time.

"Let's go Tuesdays," said Rob.

"Why?" said Nelly.

"It never seems half so long from Tuesday till Friday as it does
from Friday to Tuesday," said Rob.

"Why, why not?" asked Nelly.

"Oh, I don't know," said Rob. "Sunday's twice as long as any other day: I guess that's it."

"But you've got the Sunday each week," exclaimed Nelly: "it isn't any shorter from Tuesday to Tuesday than from Friday to Friday: what a silly boy! The Sunday comes in all the same. Don't you see?" Rob looked puzzled.

"I don't care," he said: "it seems ever so much shorter."

The first day that they were not to go to the mine, Rob said:—

"See here, Nell: if we can't go to the mine, let's go and see old Mr. Kleesman. His furnace must be done by this time. Perhaps he'll be making an assay to-day."

"Oh, good!" said Nelly. "I declare I'd almost forgotten all about him: hadn't you?"

"No, indeed!" said Rob: "I liked the mine better; but let's go there to-day."

When they reached Mr. Kleesman's steps Rob sprang up, two steps at a time.

Mr. Kleesman was very glad to see Nelly.

"I haf miss you for many days," he said. "Vy is it you not come more to see assay?"

"We have been very busy," said Nelly: "and have not stayed in town any longer than we needed to sell our things."

"I know! I know!" said Mr. Kleesman: "you haf been at the Goot Luck mine!"

"Why, who told you about it?" exclaimed Rob.

"Ach!" said Mr. Kleesman, "you tink dat mines be to be hid in dis town? Not von but knows of 'Goot Luck,' dat the little maid-child haf found;" and he looked at Nelly and smiled affectionately. "And not von but iss glad," he added, patting her on the head.

Then he turned to an old man who had come in with the children, and said, politely:—

"Vat can I do for you, sir?"

The man took off his hat and sat down, and pulled out of his pocket a little bag of stones, and threw it on the table.

"Tell me if that's worth any thing," he said.

Mr. Kleesman took a small stone out of the bag, and called:—
"Franz! Franz!"

Franz was Mr. Kleesman's servant. He tended the fires, and pounded up the stones fine in an iron mortar, and did all Mr. Kleesman's errands.

Franz came running; and Mr. Kleesman gave him the stone, and said something to him in German. Franz took the stone, and disappeared in the back room.

"After he haf make it fine," said Mr. Kleesman, "I shall assay it for you." Then, turning to Nelly and Rob, he said:—

"Can you stay? I make three assay now in three cups."

"Yes. indeed, we can!" said Nelly: "thank you! That is what we came for. We thought the furnace must be mended by this time."

While Franz was pounding the stone, the old man told Mr. Kleesman about his mine. Nelly listened with attentive ears to all he said: but Rob was busy studying the pretty little brass scales in the glass box. The man said that he and two other men had been at work for some months at this mine. The other two men were sure the ore was good; one of them had tried it with the blow-pipe, he said, and got plenty of silver.

"But I just made up my mind," said the man, "that, before I put any more money in there, I'd come to somebody that knew. I ain't such a sodhead as to think I can tell so well about things as a man that's studied 'em all his life; and I asked all about, and they all said, 'Kleesman's the man: he'd give you an honest assay of his own mind if he could get at it and weigh it.'"

Mr. Kleesman laughed heartily. He was much pleased at this compliment to his honesty.

"Yes, I tell you all true," he said. "If it be bad, or if it be good, I tell true."

"That's what I want," said the man.

Then Franz came in with the fine-powdered stone in a paper. Mr. Kleesman took some of it and weighed it in the little brass scales. Then he took some fine-powered lead and weighed that. Then he mixed the fine lead and the powdered stone together with a knife.

"I take twelve times as much lead as there iss of the stone," he said.

"What is the lead for?" asked Nelly.

"The lead he will draw out of the stone all that are bad: you will see."

Then he put the powdered stone and the lead he had mixed together into a little clay cup, and covered it over with more of the fine-powdered lead. Then he put in a little borax.

"He helps it to melt," he said.

Then he went through into the back room, carrying this cup and two others which were standing on the table already filled with powder ready to be baked.

Rob and Nelly and the old man followed him. He opened the door of the little oven and looked in: it was glowing red hot. Then he took up each cup in tongs, and set it in the oven. When all three were in, he took some burning coals from the fire above, and put them in the mouth of the oven, in front of the cups.

"Dat iss dat cold air from door do not touch dem," he said. Then he shut the door tight, and said:—

"Now ve go back. Ve vait fifteen minute."

He held his watch in his hand, so as not to make a mistake. When the fifteen minutes were over, he opened the oven-door to let a current of cool air blow above the little cups. Nelly stood on a box, as she had before, and looked in through the queer board with holes in it for the eyes. The metal in the little cups was bubbling and as red as fire. Rob tried to look, but the heat hurt his eyes so he could not bear it.

"Ven de cold air strike the cups," said Mr. Kleesman, "then the slag are formed."

"Oh, what is slag?" cried Rob.

"All that are bad go into the slag," said Mr. Kleesman.

Then he put on a pair of thick gloves, and a hat on his head, and went close up to the fiery oven door, and took out the cups, and emptied them into little hollow places in a sheet of zinc. The instant the hot metal touched the cool zinc, it spread out into a fiery red rose.

"Oh, how lovely!" cried Nelly.

"By jingo!" said Rob.

Even while they were speaking, the bright red rose turned dark,—hardened,—and there lay three shining buttons, flat and round. Their rims looked like dark glass; and in their centres was a bright, silvery spot.

Mr. Kleesman took a hammer and pounded off all this dark, shining rim. Then he pounded the little silvery buttons which were left into the right shape to fit into some tiny little clay cups he had there. They were shaped like a flowerpot, but only about an inch high.

"Now these must bake one-half hour again," he said; and put them into the oven. Pretty soon he opened the oven-door to let the cold air in again, as he had done before. That would make all the lead go off, he said: it would melt into the little cups, and leave nothing but the pure silver behind.

"Now vatch! vatch!" he said to Nelly. "In von minute you shall see a flash in de cups, like lightning, just one second: it are de last of de lead driven avay; den all is done."

Nelly watched with all her might. Sure enough, flash! flash! flash! in all three of the cups it went; the cups were fiery red; as Mr. Kleesman took them out, they turned yellow; they looked like the yolk of a hard-boiled egg hollowed out,—and there, in the bottom of each, lay a tiny, tiny silver button! Mr. Kleesman carried them into the front room and weighed them. Two of them were heavy enough to more than weigh down the little button which was always kept in the left-hand scale. That showed that the ore had silver enough in it to make it worth while to work it. The third one was so small you could hardly see it. That was the one which belonged to the old man.

"Your ore are not wort not'ing," said Mr. Kleesman to him. Nelly looked sorrowfully at the old man's face; but he only smiled, and said:—

"Well, that's just what I've suspicioned all along. I didn't believe much in all that blow-pipe work. I'm out about a hundred dollars,—that's all,—not countin' my time any thing. It's the time I grudge more'n the money. Much obliged to ye, sir." And the philosophical old fellow handed out his five dollars to pay for the assay, and walked off as composedly as if he had had good news instead of bad.

Nelly looked very grave. She was thinking of what her father had said about Mr. Scholfield's blow-pipe.

"Perhaps Mr. Scholfield was all wrong too, just like this other man. Perhaps our mine isn't good for any thing."

Nelly's face was so long that kind-hearted Mr. Kleesman noticed it, and said:—

"You haf tired: it are too long that you look at too many t'ings. You shall sit here and be quiet."

"Oh, no, thank you," said Nelly: "I am not tired. I was only thinking."

Mr. Kleesman really loved Nelly, and it distressed him to see her look troubled. He wanted to know what troubled her; but he did not like to ask. He looked at her very sympathizingly, and did not say any thing.

"Is not a blow-pipe good for any thing to tell about silver?!" said Nelly, presently.

"Oh, ho!" thought Mr. Kleesman to himself: "now I know what the little wise maiden is thinking: it is her father's mine. It did not escape her one word which this man said."

But he replied to her question as if he had not thought any thing farther.

"Not very much: the blow-pipe cannot tell true. It tell part true: not all true."

Nelly sighed, and said:—

"Come, Rob: it is time for us to go. We are very much obliged to you for letting us see the assay. It is the most wonderful thing I ever saw. It is just like a fairy story. Come, Rob."

Rob also thanked Mr. Kleesman; and they went slowly down the steps.

"Stay! stay!" said Mr. Kleesman. "Little one, vill you not ask your father that he send me some of the ore from the Goot Luck Mine? I shall assay it for you, and I vill tell you true how much silver there should come from each ton, that you are not cheated at the mill vere dey take your ore to make in de silver brick."

Nelly ran back to Mr. Kleesman, and took his hand in hers.

"Oh, thank you! thank you!" she said: "that was what I was thinking about. I was thinking what if our mine should turn out like that man's that was here this morning."

"Oh, no: I t'ink not. Every von say it iss goot, very goot," said Mr. Kleesman. "But I like to make assay. You tell your father I make it for noting: I make it for you."

"I will tell him," said Nelly; "and I am sure he will be very glad to have you do it. I will bring some of the ore next time. Good-by!" And she and Rob ran off very fast.

Nelly had made up her mind not to tell her father any thing about Mr. Kleesman's proposal to make the assay until she could see him all alone; but she forgot to tell Rob not to speak of it; and they had hardly taken their seats at the tea-table when Rob exclaimed:—

"Papa! don't you think Mr. Kleesman says a blow-pipe isn't good for any thing to tell about silver with. And there was a man there to-day, with ore out of his mine, and it hadn't any silver at all in it,—not any to speak of,—and he thought it was splendid: he and two other men; they had tried it with a blow-pipe."

Mr. Scholfield was taking tea with the Marches this night.

He listened with a smile to all Rob said. Then he said:—

"That's just like Kleesman. He thinks nobody but he can tell any thing. It's the money he's after. I see through him. Now I know

I can make as good an assay with my blow-pipe as he can with all his little cups and saucers and gimcracks, any day."

Nelly grew very red. She did not like to hear Mr. Kleesman so spoken of. She opened her mouth to speak: then bit her lips, and remained quiet.

"What is it, Nelly?" said her father.

"Nothing, sir," replied Nelly: "only I don't think Mr. Kleesman is like that. He is very kind."

"Oh, yes, he's kind enough," said Mr. Scholfield: "he's a good-natured fellow. But it's all moonshine about his being the only one who can make assays. There's a plenty of mines working here to-day that haven't ever had any assay made except by the blow-pipe. There's no use in paying a fellow three or four or five dollars for doing what you can do yourself."

"But that man said——" began Rob.

"Be quiet now, Rob," said Mr. March. "We won't talk any more about it now."

After Mr. Scholfield had gone away, Mr. March called Nelly out of the room.

"Come walk up and down in the lane with me, Nell," he said, "and tell me all about what happened at Mr. Kleesman's."

Then Nelly told her father all about it, from beginning to end.

"Upon my word, Nell," he said, "you seem to have studied the thing carefully. I should think you could almost make an assay yourself."

"I guess I could if I had the cups and things," said Nelly: "I recollect every thing he did. But, papa, won't you let him take some ore from our mine, and let him see if it is good by his way? He won't ask us any thing: he said he was doing it every day, and he could put in one more cup as well as not. Oh, do, papa!"

"I'll think about," said Mr. March.

That night he talked it over with Mrs. March, and she was as anxious as Nelly that he should let Mr. Kleesman make the assay. This decided Mr. March; and the next morning he said to Nelly:—

"Well, Nelly, you shall have your way,—you and mamma. I will take some of the ore to your old friend. I shall go up with you to-morrow myself, and carry it. I do not like to send it by you."

"Oh, good! good!" cried Nelly, and jumped up and down, and ran away to find Rob and tell him that their father would walk into town with them the next day.

When Nelly walked into Mr. Kleesman's room, holding her father by the hand, she felt very proud. She had always thought her father handsomer and nicer to look at than any other man in the world; and, when she said to Mr. Kleesman, "Here is my father, sir," this pride was so evident in her face that it made Mr. Kleesman laugh. It did not make him love Nelly any less, however. It only made him think sadly of the little girl way off in Germany who would have just as much pride in his face as Nelly did in her father's. Mr. Kleesman's love for Nelly made him treat Mr. March like an old friend.

"I am glad to see you here," he said. "I haf for your little girl von great friendship: she iss so goot. I say often to myself, she haf goot father, goot mother. She iss not like American childs I haf seen."

Mr. March was glad to have Nelly liked; but he did not wish to have her praised in this open way. So he said, very quickly:—

"Yes, Nelly is a good girl. I have come to talk to you, Mr. Kleesman, about our mine: perhaps you have heard of it,—'The Good Luck.'"

"Yes: I hear it is goot mine, very goot," replied Mr. Kleesman. "I ask the child to bring me ore. I assay it for you. It vill be pleasure to me."

"That is what I was going to ask you to do," said Mr. March. "I would like to know the exact truth about it before I go any farther. Scholfield is pressing me to put in machinery; but I do not like to spend money on it till I am sure."

"Dat iss right," said Mr. Kleesman. "Vait! vait! It is always safe to vait. Haf you brought with you the ore?"

"Yes, I have it here," replied Mr. March, and took a small bag of it from his pocket. Mr. Kleesman examined it very carefully.

His face did not look cheerful. He took piece after piece out of the bag, and, after examining them, tossed them on the table with a dissatisfied air.

"Is it all as dis?" he said.

"Yes, about like that," replied Mr. March.

Nelly watched Mr. Kleesman's face breathlessly.

"I know he don't think it is good," she whispered to Rob.

"I cannot tell till I make assay," said Mr. Kleesman. "But I t'ink it not so very good. To-morrow I vill know. To-day I cannot do. I send you vord."

"Oh, no, you need not take that trouble," said Mr. March. "The children will be in day after to-morrow. They can call."

"No, I send you vord," repeated Mr. Kleesman. "I send you vord. Dere are plenty vays. I send you vord to-morrow night. Alvays men go past my door down to valley. I send you vord."

"What do you suppose is the reason he did not want us to call for it?" said Rob, as they walked down street.

"I know," said Nelly.

"What?" said Rob, sulkily. His pride was a little touched at Mr. Kleesman's having so evidently preferred to send the message by some one else rather than by them.

"Because," said Nelly, "he is so kind he doesn't want to tell us to our face the mine isn't good."

"Oh, Nell!" exclaimed Rob, in a tone of distress, "do you think it's that?"

"I know it's that," said Nelly, calmly. "It couldn't be any thing else: you'll see. He doesn't believe that ore's good for any thing. I know by his face he doesn't. I've seen him look so at ore before now."

"Oh, Nell!" cried Rob, "what'll we do if it turns out not to be good for any thing?"

"Do!" said Nelly; "why, we shall do just what we did before. But I'm awful sorry I ever told papa about the old thing. It's too mean!"

"We haven't spent any money on it: that's one good thing," said Rob.

"Yes," said Nelly; "and it's lucky we happened in at Mr. Kleesman's just when we did: there was some good luck in that, if there isn't any in the mine."

"But I don't see why you're so sure, Nell," cried Rob: "Mr. Kleesman said he couldn't tell till he tried it."

"Well, I am sure," said Nelly: "just as sure's any thing. I know Mr. Kleesman thinks it isn't good for any thing; and if he thinks so just by looking at the stone, won't he think so a great deal more when he has burnt all the bad stuff away?"

"Well, anyhow, I shan't give up till he sends 'vord,' as he calls it," said Rob. "I guess it'll be good for a little if it isn't for much. Everybody says Mr. Scholfield knows all about mines."

"You'll see!" was all Nelly replied; and she trudged along with a very grave and set look on her face. Mr. March was to stay in town later, to see some farmers who were coming in from the country: so the children had a lonely walk home.

When it drew near to sunset, the time at which the farmers who had been up into Rosita usually returned into the valley, Rob and Nelly went down the lane to the gate, to watch for the messenger from Mr. Kleesman. The sun set, and the twilight deepened into dusk, and no messenger came. Several farm wagons passed; and, as each one approached, the children's hearts began to beat quicker, thinking that the wagon would stop, and the man would hand out a letter; but wagon after wagon passed,—and no letter. At last Nelly said:—

"It is so dark we really must go in, Rob. I don't believe it's coming to-night."

"Perhaps his furnace is broken again, and he couldn't do it to-day," said Rob.

"Perhaps so," said Nelly, drearily. "Oh, dear! I wish the old mine was in Guinea. Weren't we happier without it, Rob?"

"Yes, lots!" said Rob; "and we're making a good lot of money off the butter and eggs. I don't care about the old mine."

"I do!" said Nelly: "if it was a good mine—if it were a good mine, I mean, because then we could all have every thing we want, and papa wouldn't have to work. But I know this mine isn't a good one, and I ain't ever going to look for another's long as I live. Nor I won't tell of one, if I find it, either!"

"Pshaw, Nell! don't be a goose," said Rob. "If this one isn't good for any thing, it don't prove that the next one won't be. I'll find all I can, and try 'em one after the other."

"Well, you may: I won't!" said Nelly.

Bedtime came: still no letter. All through the evening, the children were listening so closely for the sound of wheels, that they could not attend to any thing else. Even Mr. March found it rather hard to keep his thoughts from wandering down the lane in expectation of the message from Rosita. But it did not come; and the whole family finally went to bed with their suspense unrelieved.

The next morning, while they were sitting at breakfast, and not thinking about the message at all, a man knocked at the door and handed in a letter. He had brought it from Rosita the night before, but had forgotten all about it, he said, till he was a mile past the house; and he thought as he would be going in again early in the morning, it would do as well to bring it then.

"Oh, certainly, certainly!" said Mr. March: "it was not on any pressing business. Much obliged to you, sir. Sit down and have some breakfast with us: won't you?"

The man was an old bachelor,—a Mr. Bangs,—who lived alone on a farm some six miles north of Mr. March's. He looked longingly at the nice breakfast, and said to Mrs. March:—

"Well, I had what I called a breakfast before I left home; but your coffee does smell so tempting, I think I'll take a cup,—since you're so kind."

Then he drew up a chair and sat down, and began to eat and drink as if he had just come starved from a shipwreck.

Mr. March laid the letter down by his plate, and went on talking with Mr. Bangs as politely as if he had nothing else to do.

Rob and Nelly looked at the letter; then at each other; then at their father and mother: Rob fidgeted on his chair. Finally, Nelly put down her knife and fork, and said she did not want any more breakfast. Mrs. March could hardly keep from laughing to see the children's impatience, though she felt nearly as impatient herself. At last she said to the children:—

"You may be excused, children. Run out into the barn and see if you can find any eggs!" Rob and Nelly darted off, only too glad to be free.

"Did you ever see such a pig!" exclaimed Rob. "He'd had his breakfast at home? I don't see what made papa ask him!"

"He ate as if he were half starved," said Nelly. "I guess old bachelors don't cook much that's good. Oh! I do wish he'd hurry."

Mr. Bangs had no idea of hurrying. It was a long time since he had tasted good home-made bread and butter and coffee, and he knew it would be a still longer time before he tasted them again. He almost wished he had two stomachs, like a camel, and could fill them both. At last, when he really could eat no more, and Mrs. March had poured out for him the last drop out of the coffee-pot, he went away. The children were watching in the barn to see him go. As soon as he had passed the barn-door, they scampered back to the house.

Their father had the open letter under his hand, on the table. He was looking at their mother, and there were tears in her eyes. He turned to the children, and said, in a voice which he tried hard to make cheerful:—

"Well, Nelly, are you ready for bad news?"

"Oh, yes!" interrupted Nelly, "indeed I am, all ready. I knew it would be bad news! I knew it when we were at Mr. Kleesman's."

"Pshaw!" said Rob, and sat down in a chair, and twirled his hat over and over between his knees: "I don't care! I'm going fishing." And he jumped up suddenly, and ran out of the room.

Mrs. March laughed in spite of herself.

"That is to hide how badly he feels," she said. "Let's all go fishing."

Nelly did not laugh. She stood still by the table, leaning on it.

"It's all my fault," she said. "If I hadn't found the mine, we shouldn't have had all this trouble."

"Why, child, this isn't trouble," exclaimed her father: "don't feel so. Of course we're all a little disappointed."

"A good deal!" interrupted Mrs. March, smiling.

"Yes, a good deal," he continued; "but we won't be unhappy long about it. We're no worse off than we were before. And there's one thing: we are very lucky to have got out of it so soon,—before we had put any money into it."

"What does Mr. Kleesman say?" asked Nelly.

"He says that there is a little silver in the ore, but not enough to make it pay to work the mine," replied her father; "and he says that he is more sorry to say this than he has ever been before in his life to say that ore was not good. I will read you the letter."

Then Mr. March read the whole letter aloud to Nelly. The last sentence was a droll one. Mr. Kleesman said:— "I have for your little girl so great love that I do wish she may never have more sorrow as this."

"What does he mean, papa?" asked Nelly.

"Why, he means that he hopes this disappointment about the mine will be the most serious sorrow you will ever know: that nothing worse will ever happen to you," replied Mr. March.

"Oh," said Nelly, "is that it? I couldn't make it mean any thing. Well, I hope so too."

"So do I," said Mrs. March.

"And I," said Mr. March. "And if nothing worse ever does happen to us than to think for a few weeks we have found a fortune, and then to find that we haven't, we shall be very lucky people."

So they all tried to comfort each other, and to conceal how much disappointed they really were; but all the time, each one of them was very unhappy, and knew perfectly well that all the rest were too. Mr. March was the unhappiest of the four. He had made such fine plans for the future: how he would send Rob and Nelly to school at the East; build a pretty new house; have a nice, comfortable carriage; buy all the books he wanted. Poor Mr. March! it was a very hard thing to have so many air-castles tumble down all in one minute!

Mrs. March did not mind it so much, because she had never from the beginning had very firm faith in the mine. And for Rob and Nelly it was not nearly so hard, for they had not made any definite plans of what they would like to do; and they were so young that each day brought them new pleasures in their simple life.

Colorado Snow-Birds

Jackson began her writing career as a poet and continued to write poems throughout her life. She was inspired to write "Colorado Snow-Birds" after observing the birds that often appeared near her home after a snowstorm. She began her poem by describing these birds and their behavior, but she closed it on a spiritual note. This poem first appeared in the April 1975 issue of ST. NICHOLAS.

I'll tell you how the snow-birds come,
      Here in our Winter days;
They make me think of chickens,
      With their cunning little ways.

We go to bed at night, and leave
      The ground all bare and brown,
And not a single snow-bird
      To be seen in all the town.

But when we wake at morning
      The ground with snow is white,
And with the snow, the snow-birds
      Must have traveled all the night;

For the streets and yards are full of them,
      The dainty little things,
With snow-white breasts, and soft brown heads
      And speckled russet wings.

Not here and there a snow-bird,
     As we see them at the East,
But in great flocks, like grasshoppers,
     By hundreds, at the least.

They push and crowd and jostle,
     And twitter as they feed,
And hardly lift their heads up
     For fear to miss a seed.

What 't is they eat, nobody seems
     To know or understand;
The seeds are much too fine to see,
     All sifted in the sand.

But winds last Summer scattered them,
     All thickly on these plains;
The little snow-birds have no barns,
     But God protects their grains.

They let us come quite near them,
     And show no sign of dread;
Then, in a twinkling, the whole flock
     Will flutter on ahead.

A step or two, and light, and feed,
     And look demure and tame,
And then fly again, and stop,
     As if it were a game.

Some flocks count up to thousands,
     I know, and when they fly,
Their tiny wings make rustle,
     As if a wind went by.

They go as quickly as they come,
     Go in a night or day;
Soon as the snow has melted off,
     The darlings fly away,

But come again, again, again,
     All Winter, with each snow;
Brave little armies, through the cold,
     Swift back and forth they go.

I always wondered where they lived
     In Summer, till last year
I stumbled on them in their home,
     High in the upper air;

'Way up among the clouds it was,
     A many thousand feet,
But on the mountain-side gay flowers
     Were blooming fresh and sweet.

Great pine-trees' swaying branches
     Gave cool and fragrant shade;
And here, we found, the snow-birds
     Their Summer home had made.

"Oh, ye lucky little snow-birds,"
     We said, "to know so well,
In Summer time and Winter time,
     Your destined place to dwell—

"To journey, nothing doubting,
     Down to the barren plains.
Where harvests are all over,
     To find your garnered grains!

"Oh, precious little snow-birds,
    If we were half as wise,
If we were half as trusting
    To the Father in the skies—

"He would feed us, though the harvests
    Had ceased throughout the land,
And hold us, all our lifetime,
    In the hollow of His hand!"

POEMS
BY
HELEN JACKSON

Cheyenne Mountain

Of the hundreds of poems that Jackson wrote, "Cheyenne Mountain" is one of only a few that deals directly with a specific place in Colorado. This poem originally ran in the July 31, 1879, issue of the NEW YORK INDEPENDENT. It was later included in Jackson's posthumously published collection SONNETS AND LYRICS, which Roberts Brothers released in 1886.

By easy slope to west as if it had
    No thought, when first its soaring was begun,
Except to look devoutly to the sun,
    It rises and has risen, until glad,
With light as with a garment, it is clad,
    Each dawn, before the tardy plains have won
One ray; and after day has long been done
    For us, the light doth cling reluctant, sad to leave its brow.
Beloved mountain, I
    Thy worshipper as thou the sun's, each morn
My dawn, before the dawn, receive from thee;
    And think, as thy rose-tinted peaks I see
That thou wert great when Homer was not born.
    And ere thou change all human song shall die!

HELEN HUNT JACKSON: *Selected Colorado Writings*

Helen Hunt Jackson's Colorado Writings

Bits of Travel at Home. Boston: Roberts Brothers, 1878.

"Bowlder Canyon." *New York Independent,* 21 October 1875. Included in
   Bits of Travel at Home.

"A Calendar of Sunrises in Colorado." *New York Independent,* 28 March 1874.
   Included in *Bits of Travel at Home.*

"Central City and Bob Tail Tunnel." *New York Independent,* 30 July 1874.
   Included in *Bits of Travel at Home.*

"Cheyenne Canyon." *New York Independent,* 27 August 1874.
   Included in *Bits of Travel at Home.*

"Cheyenne Mountain" (poem). *New York Independent,* 31 July 1879.

"A Colorado Road." *Atlantic Monthly,* December 1876. Included in
   Bits of Travel at Home under the title "Our New Road."

"The Colorado Snow Birds" (poem). *St. Nicholas,* April 1875.

"Colorado Springs." *New York Independent,* 13 August 1874.
   Included in *Bits of Travel at Home.*

"A Colorado Week." *New York Independent,* 1, 8, 15, 22 October 1874.
   Included in *Bits of Travel at Home.*

"A Colorado Woman's Museum." *St. Nicholas,* October 1876.

"The Cradle of Peace." *New York Independent,* 24 September 1874.
   Included in *Bits of Travel at Home.*

"Estes Park." *Christian Union,* 29 June 1882.

"Georgetown and the Terrible Mine." *New York Independent,*
   10 September 1874. Included in *Bits of Travel at Home.*

"The Grand Canyon of the Arkansas." *New York Independent,* 1 July 1875.
   Included in *Bits of Travel at Home.*

"Health Resorts in Colorado." *Youth's Companion,* 13 May 1880.

"Health-Seeking in Colorado." *Youth's Companion,* 6 May 1880.

"The Kansas and Colorado Buildings at the Centennial Exposition."
    New York Independent, 12 October 1876.

"Little Rose and the House of the Snowy Range." *Scribner's Monthly Magazine,*
    May 1878. Included in *Bits of Travel at Home.*

Nelly's Silver Mine: A Story of Colorado Life. Boston: Roberts Brothers, 1878.

"A New Anvil Chorus." *Scribner's Monthly Magazine,* January 1878.
    Included in *Bits of Travel at Home.*

"North Cheyenne Canyon." *New York Independent,* 24 March 1877.
    Included in *Bits of Travel at Home.*

"The Procession of Flowers in Colorado." *Atlantic Monthly,* October 1877.
    Included in *Bits of Travel at Home.*

"Ranch Life in Colorado." *Youth's Companion,* 20 May 1880.

"A Study of Red Canyon." *New York Independent,* 9 August 1877.
    Included in *Bits of Travel at Home.*

"A Symphony in Yellow and Red," *Atlantic Monthly,* December 1875.
    Included in *Bits of Travel at Home.*

"To Leadville." *Atlantic Monthly,* May 1879.

"A Trip into Gunnison Country." *New York Independent,* 29 December 1881.

"Wa-Ha-Toy-A: Before the Graders." *Atlantic Monthly,* June 1877.
    Included in *Bits of Travel at Home.*

"A Winter Morning at Colorado Springs." *New York Independent,*
    25 June 1874. Included in *Bits of Travel at Home.*

Selected Secondary Sources

Banning, Evelyn I. *Helen Hunt Jackson.* New York: Vanguard, 1973.

Byers, John R. and Elizabeth S. Byers. "Helen Hunt Jackson (1830-1885): Critical Bibliography of Secondary Comment." *American Literary Realism, 1870-1910,* 6 (Summer 1973): 197-241.

Eberhart, Perry. *Guide to the Colorado Ghost Towns and Mining Camps.* Denver: Sage Books, 1959.

McConnell, Virginia. "H.H., Colorado, and the Indian Problem." *Journal of the West,* 12 (April 1973): 272-280.

Mathes, Vallerie Sherer. *Helen Hunt Jackson and Her Indian Reform Legacy.* Austin: University of Texas Press, 1990.

—. *The Indian Reform Letters of Helen Hunt Jackson, 1879-1885.* Norman: University of Oklahoma Press, 1998.

Odell, Ruth. *Helen Hunt Jackson.* New York: D. Appleton-Century Co., 1939.

West, Mark I. *Wellsprings of Imagination: The Homes of Children's Authors.* New York: Neal-Schuman, 1992.

Wilcox, Rhoda D. "Helen Hunt Jackson, Outstanding Early Resident." *Colorado Springs Gazette Telegraph,* 31 December 1961.